THE QUALITY SYSTEM DEVELOPMENT HANDBOOK

WITH ISO 9002

THE QUALITY SYSTEM DEVELOPMENT HANDBOOK

WITH ISO 9002

P.S. WILTON
Q.A. Management Services Pty. Ltd.

PRENTICE HALL
New York London Toronto Sydney Tokyo Singapore

First published 1994 by
Prentice Hall
Simon & Schuster (Asia) Pte Ltd
Alexandra Distripark
Block 4, #04-31
Pasir Panjang Road
Singapore 0511

Printed in Singapore

2 3 4 5 98 97 96 95 94

ISBN 0-13-127259-4

Prentice Hall International (UK) Limited, *London*
Prentice Hall of Australia Pty. Limited, *Sydney*
Prentice Hall Canada Inc., *Toronto*
Prentice Hall Hispanoamericana, S.A., *Mexico*
Prentice Hall of India Private Limited, *New Delhi*
Prentice Hall of Japan, Inc., *Tokyo*
Editora Prentice Hall do Brasil, Ltda., *Rio de Janeiro*
Prentice Hall, Inc., Englewood Cliffs, *New Jersey*

CONTENTS

PREFACE

Understanding quality management and in particular the ISO 9000 standards has proved a major stumbling block for companies who have decided to go along the path of certification.

Q.A. Management Services Pty. Ltd. made a decision to develop, for industry, an alternative product to "full" consultancy service because we had identified that a high proportion of potential clients were being "put off" by the high cost of engaging consultants.

Our marketing found that what the majority of companies needed *initially* to satisfy their clients were a quality policy manual and example procedures.

This response posed a problem because we had earlier made a policy decision not to become involved in selling "off the shelf" quality policy manuals without awareness training regarding the meaning of quality and information concerning what else was involved in developing a quality system in the knowledge that a quality policy manual in the hands of someone with little knowledge was worthless.

We considered the costing structure of producing a quality policy manual and associated procedures and decided to produce a handbook which fully explained the terms used by quality practitioners and took the reader step by step through all the activities necessary for a company to plan, prepare, develop and implement the documentation necessary for ISO 9000 and then gain certification.

In fact we studied our own techniques for assisting companies and what we have produced in the "handbook" constitutes the way in which we would tackle the work for a client.

The package includes, we believe, all that is necessary, with a small amount of consultancy time, to guide a company through the seven steps leading to certification.

This handbook has been developed through many hours of deliberation and careful wording so that it is easily understood by all readers.

The author would like to acknowledge the help of Jean Preston who helped with the initial manuscript and the willing contributions by my fellow director Nick Travaglini. A special acknowledgment would be appropriate to Josef Lock and Q.A. Technology without whose special input and determination this book would not have been published.

P.S. Wilton
Managing Director

INTRODUCTION

1.0 UNDERSTANDING "QUALITY"

"Quality" is a word which is on everyone's lips. Definitions of "quality" jump out from textbooks, seminar presentations, course notes and consultancy packages – not necessarily concurring definitions either! "Quality" terminology abounds: total quality management (TQM), quality assurance (QA), quality control (QC), quality systems, quality manuals, etc. Not surprisingly, many people are confused by the definitions and by the terminology and may even feel too intimidated (or saturated) to give clear thought to the concept of quality in their own working environment.

The purpose of this introductory section is not to coin yet another series of "authoritative" interpretations but to try to simplify the picture and to relate the concepts to the typical company which will use this package. For the sake of consistency, we make reference to the definitions which are given in the international standard ISO 8402-1986, *Quality – Vocabulary*.

1.1 Quality

Quality: the totality of features and characteristics of a product or service that bear on its ability to satisfy stated or implied needs (ISO 8402-1986).

In the context of supplying, providing or delivering products and services there is general agreement that "quality" means "what the customer wants", i.e. that the product or service should satisfy customer perceptions and expectations both at the time of purchase and, if a product, during its useful life. This means not less than and not more than the given need. The misconception which many people hold is

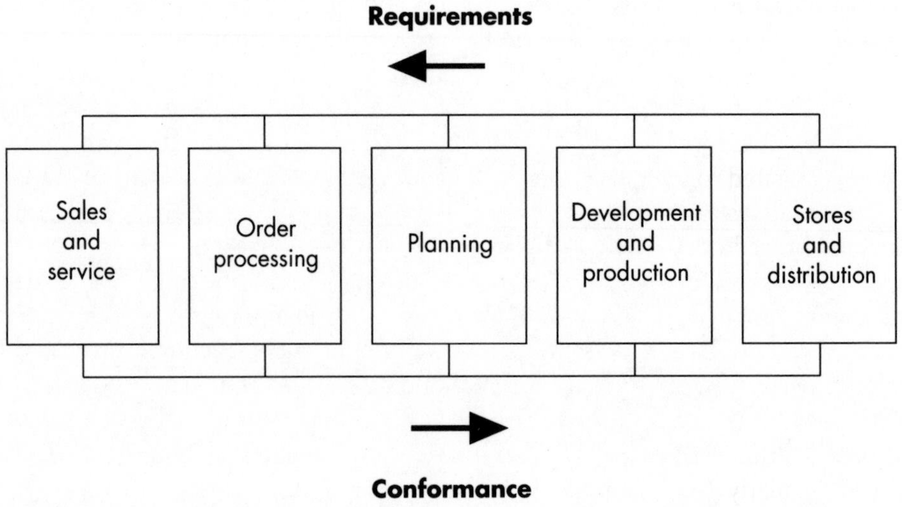
Requirements
Sales and service
Order processing
Planning
Development and production
Stores and distribution
Conformance

Figure 1 Supplier/customer interfaces within a typical organisation

that quality implies a degree of excellence or a grade – this often results from a production-oriented rather than a customer-oriented approach.

In understanding "what the customer wants", factors such as availability, delivery, servicing and price are just as important as the design and use of the product or service. These factors are normally translated into a "specification" in a contractual situation.

Everyone in the company has a role to play in assessing and satisfying the needs not only of the ultimate customer but also the needs of the intermediate "customers" within the company, e.g. production department as a customer of the stores and distribution department. This reinforces the principle behind the well-used phrase: "Quality is everybody's business."

Figure 1 illustrates the supplier/customer interfaces within a typical organisation.

1.2 Quality Assurance and Quality Control

> Quality assurance: all those planned and systematic actions necessary to provide adequate confidence that a product or service will satisfy given requirements for quality.
>
> Quality control: the operational techniques and activities that are used to fulfil requirements for quality.
>
> (ISO 8402-1986)

These two terms are very often confused and used incorrectly. Many companies are familiar with the term "quality control" which may have been used in the context of inspection, although that is a rather restricted interpretation. More generally, quality control is concerned with processes and operational techniques to achieve and sustain the planned quality criteria, using feedback from inspection at various stages in the process.

"Quality assurance" is concerned with providing adequate confidence (assurance) to external clients or regulatory authorities that products and services will meet stated or implied needs. This confidence comes from the objective evidence that systems and controls are in place and working effectively, i.e. quality manuals, procedures, audits and reviews.

In a typical company, an example of quality *control* might be a system (mechanical or manual) for marking products with identification tags or numbers. Quality *assurance* would be the documentation of the procedures to ensure the system works properly, that the responsibilities are correctly assigned and understood, that there is a system to check that the type of identification meets the customer's requirements (per the specification), and that the system is reviewed and audited regularly to maintain its effectiveness.

1.3 Quality System

Quality system: the organisation structure, responsibilities, procedures, processes and resources for implementing quality management (ISO 8402-1986).

Thankfully, there seems to be little or no disagreement over the definition of a quality system.

In practice, every company has systems of one sort or another in place, which may or may not be documented and, may or may not fully meet the company's quality objectives. When considering embarking on a quality programme, many companies are intimidated by the (mistaken) belief that they will have to start with a clean slate which will involve significant operational and organisational changes. Each company's quality system is unique and there is no such thing as a "model system", notwithstanding the fact that there are standards which specify the minimum requirements against which quality systems can be assessed, and certified, e.g. ISO 9000 standards.

1.4 Quality Management

Quality management: that aspect of the overall management function that determines and implements the quality policy (ISO 8402-1986).

In a literal sense, quality management is responsible for setting quality policies and objectives and providing resources to implement the quality system. This narrow definition implies that "quality" is another management function along with finance, administration, marketing, etc.

More and more emphasis is now being given to the broader concept of "total quality management" (TQM) which is based on the philosophy of quality improvement through the reduction of waste – human effort, machine time, materials and knowledge. This philosophy encompasses every individual in the organisation and promotes the concept of a quality "chain" where there is a supplier-customer relationship in every "link". As this handbook is primarily concerned with development of a quality system, TQM issues are not covered in any depth.

2.0 STANDARDS AND CERTIFICATION

Standards are used to specify the requirements against which products, processes or services are defined or assessed. Traditionally, standards were developed for particular products or processes and certification was based on conformance to design and function. An alternative form of certification is to assess a company's capabilities to consistently meet customer requirements, i.e. its systems, rather than its individual products. While the first type of certification is still very relevant in a number of cases, more and more companies are now seeking certification of their quality systems. Certification involves assessment by an independent authority against the requirements of the standards which, if acceptable, results in a certificate which provides the necessary quality assurance to the customer.

It is important to bear in mind that certification of a company's quality system does not imply any "level" or "grade" of quality (see 1.0 earlier). Neither does it assess the effectiveness of the company's total quality management. The only measure of TQM is the market-place!

2.1 Standards

Table 1 contains a list of the current international standards and guidelines related to quality systems. We have also included in the Appendix of this Introduction, extracts from the international standard ISO 8402-1986, *Quality – Vocabulary*, which complements the ISO 9000 series.

This package also contains guidelines on the selection of the most appropriate standard for your company depending on your client's requirements (see Step 1). The most common, or applicable, standard is ISO 9002 and the package is accordingly aimed mainly at those companies. Nevertheless, the principles and examples can readily be applied to quality systems of the other standards.

The *advantages* of having quality system standards are:

- clearly defined requirements so that the customer gets the necessary quality assurance;
- the establishment of minimum requirements for companies to supply quality controls and produce documentation;
- a uniform basis for comparing suppliers.

The *disadvantages* of quality system standards are:

- the perception that achievement of the required standard is the ultimate goal, whereas in fact it only lays down *minimum* requirements;
- their generic nature which sometimes makes it difficult to apply certain elements across a range of industries and types of company.

2.2 Certification

"Third-party certification" means having your company's quality system assessed by an independent body against one of the quality system standards, resulting in a certificate, if satisfactory. "Second-party assessment" by a purchaser or customer, i.e. someone who has a direct interest in your company's business, does not generally

Table 1 Quality assurance standards

Standards body (country)	Quality management and quality assurance standards: Guidelines for selection and use	Quality systems: Model for quality assurance in design/development, production, servicing	Quality systems: Model for quality assurance in production and installation	Quality systems: Model for quality assurance in final inspection and test	Quality management and quality system elements: Guidelines
ISO	ISO 9000-1987	ISO 9001-1987	ISO 9002-1987	ISO 9003-1987	ISO 9004-1987
Australia	AS 3900	AS 3901	AS 3902	AS 3903	AS 3904
Austria	OE NORM-PREN 29000	OE NORM-PREN 29001	OE NORM-PREN 29002	OE NORM-PREN 29003	OE NORM-PREN 29004
Belgium	NBN x 50-002-1	NBN x 50-003	NBN x 50-004	NBN x 50-005	NBN x 50-002-2
Canada	–	–	–	–	CSA Q420-87
China	GB/T 10300.1-88	GB/T 10300.2-88	GB/T 10300.3-88	GB/T 10300.4-88	GB/T 10300.5-88
Denmark	DS/EN 29000	DS/EN 29001	DS/EN 29002	DS/EN 29003	DS/EN 29004
Finland	SFS-ISO 9000	SFS-ISO 9001	SFS-ISO 9002	SFS-ISO 9003	SFS-ISO 9004
France	NF x 50-121	NF x 50-131	NF x 50-132	NF x 50-133	NF x 50-122
Germany (FR)	DIN ISO 9000	DIN ISO 9001	DIN ISO 9002	DIN ISO 9003	DIN ISO 9004
Hungary	MI 18990-1988	MI 18991-1988	MI 18992-1988	MI 18993-1988	MI 18994-1988
India	IS 10201 Part 2	IS 10201 Part 4	IS 10201 Part 5	IS 10201 Part 6	IS 10201 Part 3
Ireland	IS 300 Part 0/ ISO 9000	IS 300 Part 1/ ISO 9001	IS 300 Part 2/ ISO 9002	IS 300 Part 3/ ISO 9003	IS 300 Part 0/ ISO 9004
Italy	UNI/EN 29000 -1987	UNI/EN 29001 -1987	UNI/EN 29002 -1987	UNI/EN 29003 -1987	UNI/EN 29004 -1987
Malaysia	–	MS 985/ISO 9001 -1987	MS 985/ISO 9002 -1987	MS 985/ISO 9003 -1987	–
Netherlands	NEN-ISO 9000	NEN-ISO 9001	NEN-ISO 9002	NEN-ISO 9003	NEN-ISO 9004
New Zealand	NZS 5600 Part 1 -1987	NZS 5601-1987	NZS 5602-1987	NZS 5603-1987	NZS 5600 Part 2 -1987
Norway	NS-EN 29000-1988	NS-EN 29001-1988	NS-ISO 9002	NS-ISO 9003	–
South Africa	SABS 0157 Part 0	SABS 0157 Part I	SABS 0157 Part II	SABS 0157 Part III	SABS 0157 Part IV
Spain	UNE 66 900	UNE 66 901	UNE 66 902	UNE 66 903	UNE 66 904
Sweden	SS-ISO 9000-1988	SS-ISO 9001-1988	SS-ISO 9002-1988	SS-ISO 9003-1988	SS-ISO 9004-1988
Switzerland	SN-ISO 9000	SN-ISO 9001	SN-ISO 9002	SN-ISO 9003	SN-ISO 9004
Tunisia	NT 110.18-1987	NT 110.19-1987	NT 110.20-1987	NT 110.21-1987	NT 110.22-1987
United Kingdom	BS 5750-1987 Part 0 Section 0.1 ISO 9000/ EN 29000	BS 5750-1987 Part 1 ISO 9001/ EN 29001	BS 5750-1987 Part 2 ISO 9002/ EN 29002	BS 5750-1987 Part 3 ISO 9003/ EN 29003	BS 5750-1987 Part 0 ISO 9004/ EN 29004
USA	ANSI/ASQC Q90	ANSI/ASQC Q91	ANSI/ASQC Q92	ANSI/ASQC Q93	ANSI/ASQC Q94
USSR	–	40.9001-88	40.9002-88	–	–
Yugoslavia	JUS A.K. 1.010	JUS A.K. 1.012	JUS A.K. 1.013	JUS A.K. 1.014	JUS A.K. 1.011
European Community	EN 29000	EN 29001	EN 29002	EN 29003	EN 29004

result in a certificate. We have used the term "assessor" to mean the third party certification body.

Some of the main, internationally recognised, third-party certification bodies include:

- Lloyds Register;
- Bureau Veritas;
- Det Norske Veritas; and
- in most countries, the national standards organisation also operates in a separate capacity as an assessor, e.g. SIRIM (Malaysia); SISIR (Singapore); BS (United Kingdom).

All of these bodies charge fees for the certification process, depending on the size of the company and the scope of the certification. The choice of assessor may also depend on the industry involved.

The certification process is normally undertaken in two stages:

- Documentation review and pre-assessment visit
- Final assessment (on site)

The process and timescales, etc., are covered in more detail in Step 7 of the handbook.

A certificate is issued, stating the standard and scope of the assessment and it is valid for three years. The certificate also bears the certification "mark" of the assessor and you are entitled to use that mark on company literature. During the three-year period, surveillance audits will be carried out (normally two a year) to ensure the required standards are being maintained.

3.0 THE COST OF QUALITY

There is another, much-debated misconception about quality: that it is too "costly" to implement or that it is some kind of luxury which the company cannot afford. This type of thinking usually comes from the perception of "levels" or "grades" of quality rather than quality in the sense of fitness for purpose. The smart answer, of course, is that companies cannot afford *not* to implement effective quality systems!

The subject of quality costs is complex and detailed and is only touched on briefly here, to provoke further thoughts. Quality costs can be split into *direct* costs, which appear in one form or another in the company's accounts, and *indirect* costs, which relate to the company's position in the market-place.

Direct costs can be split into three main categories:

- Prevention costs – planning, control, verification, auditing, training, etc.
- Appraisal costs – inspection, evaluation, reporting.
- Failure costs – *internal* costs, such as rejects, reworks, defects diagnosis, etc.
  – *external* costs, such as customer complaints/refunds, returned goods, etc.

Studies have found that these direct costs alone can often amount to 30 per cent of a company's total revenue. These studies have also found a direct correlation between high total quality costs and low prevention costs. Investment in an effective quality system to prevent failures can have extremely high returns. Figure 2 shows how expenditure can be revised to produce cost savings in a typical company.

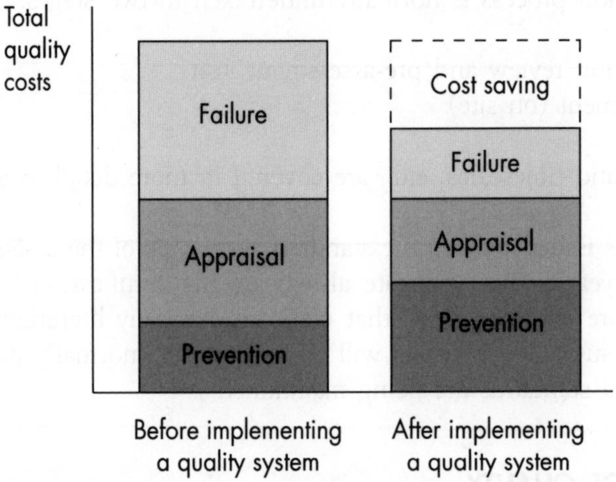
Total quality costs
Failure
Appraisal
Prevention
Cost saving
Failure
Appraisal
Prevention
Before implementing a quality system
After implementing a quality system

Figure 2 Implementing an effective quality system results in cost saving

Indirect costs are less easy to categorise and to measure but they include:

- loss of sales through dissatisfied customers;
- loss of market share to quality-oriented competitors;
- lost opportunities to maximise employee productivity through motivation and commitment;
- warranty and liability costs.

The "iceberg theory" shown in Figure 3 is vividly relevant in this context, i.e. that the majority of quality-related losses occur below the surface and are not readily visible.

Implementation of a quality system to an ISO 9000 series standard is not guaranteed to instantly transform your company's profitability and the benefits must be looked upon as long-term. They are undoubtedly recurring and improving. In the short-term, there are obviously costs associated with getting a quality system in place and having it certified, if necessary. These costs are listed in sections 3.1–3.4.

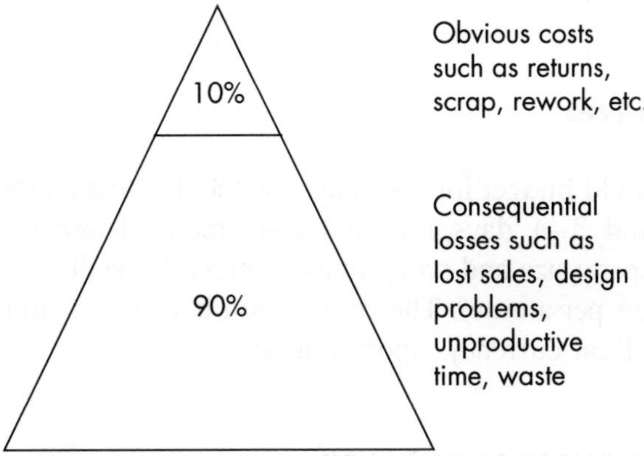
10%
Obvious costs such as returns, scrap, rework, etc.
90%
Consequential losses such as lost sales, design problems, unproductive time, waste

Figure 3 The iceberg theory

3.1 Manhours and Equipment

As a general guideline, you should budget for 25–35 manhours per week for a period of 12–18 months. This comprises the time of your delegated "quality manager" as well as all other personnel assisting in developing and implementing procedures, etc. (*Note:* Your quality manager does not have to undertake this role on a full-time basis – see Step 1.) It is unlikely that you will significantly reduce the 12–18 month period simply by allocating more time per week as it takes time for the system to be implemented and tested.

Equipment costs will probably be minimal, e.g. additional inspection/test equipment, filing facilities, stationery, etc.

3.2 Education and Training

Step 4 of the handbook emphasises the importance of education and training and promotion of "quality awareness" amongst the workforce. Such costs may be incurred through in-house training (informal and/or structured courses) and externally run courses. It is difficult to give guidelines on the extent of these costs as each company has different requirements. Nevertheless each company should be prepared to allocate sufficient time for every member of the workforce to participate in quality awareness programmes.

3.3 Consultancy Assistance

Although this is primarily a "do-it-yourself" package, from time to time expert assistance may be required and, in fact, is advisable as a means of ensuring that you are on the right track. Such consultancy assistance can include reviewing the quality policy manual and procedures, conducting quality awareness training and providing support during the certification process, if necessary.

3.4 Certification Fees

As a guide, you should budget for 2–3 days for the documentation review and pre-assessment visit and 3–4 days for final assessment. These estimates will vary depending on company size and scope of assessment. Surveillance visits will usually amount to 3–4 days per annum. The certification bodies can supply man-day rates and fixed costs in local currency, upon request.

4.0 THE "DO-IT-YOURSELF" PACKAGE

We have been assisting clients to develop and implement quality systems and assess their effectiveness for many years. Historically, the companies that have sought our assistance have been forward-thinking, pro-active companies that have recognised the benefits of gaining a competitive edge by producing goods and services which *consistently* meet their customers' needs.

For a variety of reasons, many companies do not want to engage the services of a full-time, or part-time consultant to assist in developing and implementing their quality system. The reason may be one of cost; it may be one of expertise: suitably experienced and qualified people already in the company; or it may be one of involvement: the long-term benefits of "learning by experience". While, as consultants, we would naturally argue that our services are cost-effective, expert and interactive, we do recognise that there is a market for a package which will guide management, step-by-step, in the development and implementation of their own quality system. Hence this "DIY" package (handbook).

4.1 Making Best Use of the Handbook

The step-by-step approach is basically the approach we follow ourselves in assisting clients. The handbook provides all of the guidelines on how we would plan and implement the work in your company and contains many relevant examples.

Some words of caution, however:

- The success of the whole exercise is totally dependent upon the knowledge and enthusiasm and commitment of everyone in the company, particularly management. As discussed in Step 1, the choice of person to lead and manage the work is a crucial factor.
- The package has been prepared on a general basis so that it can be used by a variety of companies. Therefore, take great care and time when considering examples and relate the elements of the system to your own operations. The system will be audited to verify that you actually do what the documentation states, so there is little point in merely adapting someone else's procedures!
- Allow sufficient time for the quality manual and procedures to be discussed, written, reviewed, tested and implemented. On the other hand, do not try to radically change your operations unless you are convinced you need to. Make the most of what you already have in the way of methods and systems.

5.0 CONTENTS OF THE 7-STEP PACKAGE

Step 1: Management Commitment
Step 2: Quality System Requirements and the Quality Policy Manual
Step 3: Planning
Step 4: Training, Education and Quality Awareness
Step 5: Procedures
Step 6: Auditing
Step 7: Certification

INTRODUCTION

Appendix ISO 8402-1986 (Extracts)

TERMS AND DEFINITIONS

The following definitions are extracted from the international standard, ISO 8402 entitled *Quality Vocabulary*. These definitions directly apply to the ISO 9000 standards on quality management and quality systems.

In this international standard, unless otherwise stated, "product" or "service" may be:

- the result of activities or processes (tangible product, intangible product, such as a service, a computer program, a design, directions for use); or
- an activity or process (such as the provision of a service or the execution of a production process).

1. QUALITY

The totality of features and characteristics of a product or service that bear on its ability to satisfy stated or implied needs.

Notes:

(a) In a contractual environment, needs are specified, whereas in other environments, implied needs should be identified and defined.
(b) In many instances, needs can change with time; this implies periodic revision of specifications.
(c) Needs are usually translated into features and characteristics with specified criteria. Needs may include aspects of useability, safety, availability, reliability, maintainability, economics and environment.
(d) The term "quality" is not used to express a degree of excellence in a comparative sense nor is it used in a quantitative sense for technical evaluations. In these cases a qualifying adjective shall be used. For example, use can be made of the following terms:
   - "relative quality" where products or services are ranked on a relative basis in the "degree of excellence" or "comparative" sense;
   - "quality level" and "quality measure" where precise technical evaluations are carried out in a "quantitative sense".
(e) Product or service quality is influenced by many stages of interactive activities, such as design, production or service operation and maintenance.
(f) The economic achievement of satisfactory quality involves all stages of the quality loop (quality spiral) as a whole. The contributions to quality of the various stages within the quality loop (quality spiral) are sometimes identified separately for emphasis. Two examples are "quality attributable to design" and "quality attributable to implementation".

(g) In some reference sources, "quality" is referred to as "fitness for use", "fitness for purpose", "customer satisfaction" or "conformance to the requirements". Since these represent only certain facets of quality, fuller explanations are usually required that eventually lead to the concept defined earlier.

2. GRADE

An indicator of category or rank related to features or characteristics that cover different sets of needs for products or services intended for the same functional use.

Notes:

(a) Grade reflects a planned difference in requirements or, if not planned, a recognised difference. The emphasis is on the functional use/cost relationship.
(b) A high grade article can be of inadequate quality as far as satisfying needs and vice versa, e.g. a luxurious hotel with poor service or a small guest-house with excellent service.
(c) Where grade is denoted numerically, it is common for the highest grade to be 1 and the lower grades to be 2, 3, 4, etc. Where grade is denoted by a points score, for example by a number of stars, the lowest grade usually has the fewest points or stars.

3. QUALITY LOOP (QUALITY SPIRAL)

Conceptual model of interacting activities that influence the quality of a product or service in the various stages ranging from the identification of needs to the assessment of whether these needs have been satisfied.

4. QUALITY POLICY

The overall quality intentions and direction of an organisation as regards quality, as formally expressed by top management.

Note: The quality policy forms one element of the corporate policy and is authorised by top management.

5. QUALITY MANAGEMENT

That aspect of the overall management function that determines and implements the quality policy.

Notes:

(a) The attainment of desired quality requires the commitment and participation of all members of the organisation whereas the responsibility for quality management belongs to top management.

(b) Quality management includes strategic planning, allocation of resources and other systematic activities for quality such as quality planning, operations and evaluations.

6. QUALITY ASSURANCE

All those planned and systematic actions necessary to provide adequate confidence that a product or service will satisfy given requirements for quality.

Notes:

(a) Unless given requirements fully reflect the needs of the user, quality assurance will not be complete.

(b) For effectiveness, quality assurance usually requires a continuing evaluation of factors that affect the adequacy of the design or specification for intended applications as well as verifications and audits of production, installation and inspection operations. Providing confidence may involve producing evidence.

(c) Within an organisation, quality assurance serves as a management tool. In contractual situations, quality assurance also serves to provide confidence in the supplier.

7. QUALITY CONTROL

The operational techniques and activities that are used to fulfil requirements for quality.

Notes:

(a) In order to avoid confusion, care should be taken to include a modifying term when referring to a sub-set of quality control such as "manufacturing quality control", or when referring to a broader concept, such as "company-wide quality control".

(b) Quality control involves operational techniques and activities aimed both at monitoring a process and at eliminating causes of unsatisfactory performance at relevant stages of the quality loop (quality spiral) in order to result in economic effectiveness.

8. QUALITY SYSTEM

The organisational structure, responsibilities, procedures, processes and resources for implementing quality management.

Notes:

(a) The quality system should only be as comprehensive as is needed to meet the quality objectives.
(b) For contractual, mandatory and assessment purposes, demonstration of the implementation of identified elements in the system may be required.

9. QUALITY PLAN

A document setting out the specific quality practices, resources and sequence of activities relevant to a particular product, service, contract or project.

10. QUALITY AUDIT

A systematic and independent examination to determine whether quality activities and related results comply with planned arrangements and whether these arrangements are implemented effectively and are suitable to achieve objectives.

Notes:

(a) The quality audit typically applies, but is not limited, to a quality system or elements thereof, to processes, to products, or to services. Such audits are often called "quality system audit", "process quality audit", "product quality audit", or "service quality audit".
(b) Quality audits are carried out by staff not having direct responsibility in the areas being audited but, preferably, working in cooperation with the relevant personnel.
(c) One purpose of a quality audit is to evaluate the need for improvement or corrective action. An audit should not be confused with "surveillance" or "inspection" activities performed for the sole purpose of process control or product acceptance.
(d) Quality audits can be conducted for internal or external purposes.

11. QUALITY SURVEILLANCE

The continuing monitoring and verification of the status of procedures, methods, conditions, processes, products and services, and analysis of records in relation to stated references to ensure that specified requirements for quality are being met.

Notes:

(a) Quality surveillance may be carried out by or on behalf of the customer to ensure that the contractual requirements are being met.
(b) Surveillance may have to take into account factors which can result in deterioration or degradation with time.

12. QUALITY SYSTEM REVIEW

A formal evaluation by top management of the status and adequacy of the quality system in relation to quality policy and new objectives resulting from changing circumstances.

13. DESIGN REVIEW

A formal, documented, comprehensive and systematic examination of a design to evaluate the design requirements and the capability of the design to meet these requirements and to identify problems and propose solutions.

Notes:

(a) Design review by itself is not sufficient to ensure proper design.
(b) A design review can be conducted at any stage of the design process.
(c) The capability of the design encompasses such things as fitness for purpose, feasibility, manufacturability, measurability, performance, reliability, maintainability, safety, environmental aspects, time scale and life cycle cost.
(d) Participants at each design review should include qualified staff encompassing all pertinent functions affecting quality.

14. INSPECTION

Activities such as measuring, examining, testing, gauging one or more characteristics of a product or service and comparing these with specified requirements to determine conformity.

15. TRACEABILITY

The ability to trace the history, application or location of an item or activity, or similar items or activities, by means of recorded identification.

Notes:

(a) The term "traceability" may have one of three main meanings:
- In a distribution sense, it relates to a product or service.
- In a calibration sense, it relates measuring equipment to national or international standards, primary standards or basic physical constants or properties.
- In a data collection sense, it relates calculations and data generated throughout the quality loop to a product or service.

(b) Traceability requirements should be specified for some stated period of history or to some point of origin.

16. CONCESSION (WAIVER)

Written authorisation to use or release a quantity of material, components or stores already produced but which do not conform to the specified requirements.

Note: Concessions (waivers) should be for limited quantities or periods, and for specified uses.

17. PRODUCTION PERMIT (DEVIATION PERMIT)

Written authorisation, prior to production or before provision of a service, to depart from specified requirements for a specified quantity or for a specified time.

18. RELIABILITY

The ability of an item to perform a required function under stated conditions for a stated period of time.

The term "reliability" is also used as a reliability characteristic denoting a probability of success or a success ratio.

Note: This definition is taken from IEC Publication 271; any update of this term in the Publication 271 will be considered as a replacement of this definition.

19. PRODUCT LIABILITY (SERVICE LIABILITY)

A generic term used to describe the onus on a producer or others to make restitution for loss related to personal injury, property damage or other harm caused by a product or service.

Note: The limits on liability may vary from country to country according to national legislation.

20. NONCONFORMITY

The nonfulfilment of specified requirements.

Notes:

(a) The definition covers the departure or absence of one or more quality characteristics or quality system elements from specified requirements.
(b) The basic difference between "nonconformity" and "defect" is that specified requirements may differ from the requirements for the intended use (see also note b of item 21).

21. DEFECT

The nonfulfilment of intended usage requirements.

Notes:

(a) The definition covers the departure or absence of one or more quality characteristics from intended usage requirements.
(b) The difference between "nonconformity" and "defect" is that specified requirements may differ from the requirements for the intended use (see also note b of item 20).

22. SPECIFICATION

The document that prescribes the requirements with which the product or service has to conform.

Note: A specification should refer to or include drawings, patterns or other relevant documents and should also indicate the means and the criteria whereby conformity can be checked.

ALPHABETICAL INDEX OF APPENDIX

STEP 1

MANAGEMENT COMMITMENT

Warning!!
As the success of the project to implement a quality management system is entirely dependent upon a commitment by management (because without management commitment it would be unreasonable to expect workforce commitment), this handbook can only assist where a desire exists to be the best in your particular business.

1.1 IDENTIFY CLIENT REQUIREMENTS

The objective of your company should be to provide goods or services which meet the requirements of your main clients (the terms "client" and "customer" are interchangeable throughout the handbook). These requirements may include the provision of some "assurance" that the goods or services have been produced or performed within the framework of quality control – hence, evidence being required of a quality system to a defined standard such as ISO 9001, ISO 9002 or ISO 9003.

In the first instance, you should discuss with your clients what *exactly* their requirements are because you may be contemplating a full-scale exercise to meet ISO 9001, whereas your clients may only require assurance in respect of final inspection and test (ISO 9003).

1.2 SELECT THE MOST APPROPRIATE QUALITY STANDARD

The standards which this package is aimed at are:

- ISO 9001 – Quality systems for design/development, production, installation and servicing.
- ISO 9002 – Quality systems for production and installation.
- ISO 9003 – Quality systems for final inspection and test.

Table 1 (p. 6) is a matrix showing the national equivalents of these ISO standards. ("EN" denotes the European Committee for Standardisation equivalent.) Therefore, meeting the requirements of your country's national standard automatically satisfies the requirements of ISO 9000 and other national equivalents. However, if your clients require your certificate to state another national standard, e.g. BS 5750, you will have to choose an assessor who is authorised to certify to that standard. Most of the assessors are, in fact, international bodies. Certification and the issue of certificates by third parties is discussed in more detail in the Introduction section (see 2.0) and in Step 7.

Most companies involved in manufacturing or service industries will aim for ISO 9002. However, if your company is involved in the design of products, it will be necessary to specify ISO 9001 which contains requirements for design controls.

If you have any doubts about the choice of a quality system standard, professional guidance should be sought from a reputable quality management consultant.

Note: You may be able to specify the scope of certification as applying only to certain parts of the company's operations, if that is appropriate. You will obviously then be restricted in the use of the certificate.

1.3 PREPARE THE COMPANY QUALITY POLICY STATEMENT

The company quality policy statement is the most important document produced by a company because it sets the primary quality aims and objectives of your company and is always incorporated within the quality policy manual. For practical purposes it is displayed at prominent places in the workplace (entrance area, notice boards). The quality policy statement is the means by which your company's management not only puts in writing its objectives for, and commitment to, quality, but is also the means by which you *communicate* them to the workforce, to clients and to the outside world in general.

The preparation of a quality policy statement is an individual exercise and careful thought should be given to the definition of company policies by the steering committee. A sample quality policy statement is shown on page 58 by way of a guide only as to the general format and level of detail required.

The company quality policy statement should be prepared on company stationery and signed by the managing director, or chief executive. Copies should be framed and placed in prominent positions at every site to reinforce commitment by the workforce and to indicate to your clients and visitors that *your* company is committed in every respect to quality.

1.4 ESTABLISH A STEERING COMMITTEE

A fundamental prerequisite for the development and implementation of an effective quality system is the quality awareness and commitment of the executive management. In this context the general manager should be the chairperson of a "steering committee" to provide emphasis and authority to decisions and actions emanating therefrom and to demonstrate the company's full commitment to achieving its stated quality policy and objectives.

The primary function of the steering committee is to provide direction, co-ordination and supervision of the strategies employed in putting the quality system into place. (Once the system is in place, the steering committee can be disbanded as the management review process will ensure the effectiveness of the quality system is regularly reviewed [see 1.7 later].)

Once a decision has been made to proceed with a quality system and a quality representative has been appointed, the general manager/senior executive and quality representative should familiarise themselves with this handbook and arrange at a convenient time to carry out the remaining stages of this section which should form separate topics of discussion at the first steering committee meeting.

The steering committee should also include the company's quality representative to facilitate the collation of data and the co-ordination and dissemination of information between management and the workforce.

Other members of the company may be co-opted onto the committee either on a full-time basis or as and when their sphere of influence becomes affected.

It is desirable for the steering committee to convene on a regular and frequent basis throughout the development and implementation of the quality system. Minutes of the meetings of the committee should be kept as quality records.

1.5 CHOOSE A "QUALITY REPRESENTATIVE"

The selection of a member of staff, nominated the "quality representative" to co-ordinate the development of procedures and documents, to implement and monitor the quality system and to liaise between management and the workforce is a *critical* activity in your programme.

The managing director or senior executive in the company should be responsible for deciding on the choice of the quality representative. The person chosen should be senior enough to be able to assume responsibility and authority and, at the same time, be able to deal with people at all levels within the organisation. The quality representative must have a good knowledge of the company's products or services and be given the freedom to examine all areas of the company's business to resolve quality issues. It is important to choose someone with an already active role in the company rather than someone with a low profile or someone you cannot slot into any other role.

In practical terms, the quality representative normally assumes this role alongside his* existing duties and it is therefore important for everyone in the organisation to recognise that an existing, functional reporting relationship is totally separate from that person's reporting relationship as the quality representative. For example, the purchasing manager may be selected as the quality representative: in his normal role he reports directly to the operations manager, but in the role of quality representative he reports to the steering committee which may involve more senior management than the operations manager.

1.6 COMMUNICATE COMMITMENT TO THE WORKFORCE

As we have stressed previously, management commitment is a key factor in the implementation of an effective quality system. Just as important, however, is the commitment of the rest of the workforce who will need to put the policies into practice. Too often, senior management embarks on a quality system programme, makes some grandiose policy statement, appoints a quality representative, establishes a steering committee, all without informing the workforce or unions, and then wonders why there is resistance to discussion and documenting procedures.

---

* Wherever the term "his" is used, it is intended to mean "his" or "her".

The clear lesson to be learned is that you cannot "force" a quality system into the workplace, nor can you expect a successful certification if your procedures and policies do not reflect your actual practices.

At a very early stage in the programme you should aim to give a brief presentation to the whole workforce (or a series of presentations if that is more appropriate, to allow for continued production/shift patterns, etc.) on *why* the company is embarking on the programme, *who* the key personnel are (i.e. the quality representative and the steering committee) and *what* is expected from the workforce. These presentations are often more effective through training specialists and certainly have more impact if the opening address is given by the managing director.

Step 4 is entirely devoted to training, education and quality awareness and provides more detailed guidelines on how to promote quality within the workforce.

1.7 SET UP THE MANAGEMENT REVIEW SYSTEM

One of the "requirements" or "elements" of a quality system is for a process of "management review" of the effectiveness of the system (see Step 2 for the definition of requirements and elements). This does not merely mean a review of audit findings or the reports from the steering committee as some would like to believe. The purpose of a separate management review activity is to take a much broader look at the quality system and to assess how *effective* it is in meeting management's objectives. This involves continually identifying and assessing client needs, analysing causes of system deficiencies, making sure corrective action is taken, undertaking cost/benefit analyses and reviewing resource and personnel requirements.

This type of review should be carried out independently of the developmental steering committee (although it may involve some of those members) and should take place on a regular basis, e.g. once every three or six months depending upon the size of company and amount of feedback being used during the review. It is usually possible to incorporate the management review activity into the agenda of an existing management meeting, e.g. an operations-type meeting. The reviews should be documented and minuted. The best approach is for a management review procedure to be developed.

STEP 2

QUALITY SYSTEM REQUIREMENTS AND THE QUALITY POLICY MANUAL

2.1 GENERAL INTRODUCTION

This section of the handbook is included here so that it will be read and reviewed before the more detailed steps on planning, development and implementation. The contents of this section will undoubtedly be referred to as you proceed through the steps but we recommend that you read it at least once at this stage.

The aim of this section is to explain the requirements of ISO 9002 in a simple manner, using examples to which you can relate your own company's operations. Whilst every effort has been made to detail the requirements of ISO 9002, there is no provision to cater for the ISO 9001 or ISO 9003 user. By necessity, the standards are written very generally and this can often result in misunderstandings and difficulties in interpretation.

This section is structured into two main parts:

- Explanation of quality system elements and requirements
- Guidelines on the development of a quality policy manual, including a "model" quality policy manual

Although it may seem premature to introduce the development of the quality policy manual at this stage, in practice, you will probably develop it concurrently with Steps 3, 4 and 5 of this handbook; and we believe you should be familiar with the layout and terminology typically used, before you start your training seminar and proceed to the remaining steps.

2.2 QUALITY SYSTEM ELEMENTS/REQUIREMENTS

To make effective use of this section, we suggest you refer to the relevant standard itself, i.e. ISO 9002, for the literal definition of the requirements and then read our general explanation contained here (which may be considered a reference to simplify the literal definition), in conjunction with the model quality policy manual. While our explanations are as general as possible, we have devised examples which would probably apply mainly to manufacturing or engineering companies, seeking certification to ISO 9002. (*Note:* There is an interim standard [ISO 9004.2 to ISO 9002] which provides guidelines for service companies. It is not certifiable at this stage.) Wherever possible, we have tried to relate the examples to other types of industry as well.

As you will see from the standards, ISO 9000 section 4 details the quality system requirements. There are eighteen parts to this section in ISO 9002 and each part is referred to as a system "element".

It is important to understand what is meant by a quality system "element". Our interpretation is that the term "function" could be substituted as this may be more familiar in a business context. All companies have common *functions*, e.g. control of documents (drawings, instructions, orders, etc.), purchasing (the buying of goods, raw materials or hiring of services which go into *your* final product), inspection and testing at various stages in the process or of the final finished product, etc. These functions are not necessarily associated with departments in the company, e.g. document control is common to every part of the company. Therefore, in deciding on how you will meet the requirements of the eighteen system elements, you must consider how they will affect the company as a whole.

These elements are:

ISO 9002 reference	Title
4.1	Management responsibility
4.2	Quality system
4.3	Contract review
4.4	Document control
4.5	Purchasing
4.6	Purchaser-supplied product
4.7	Product identification and traceability
4.8	Process control
4.9	Inspection and testing
4.10	Inspection, measuring and test equipment
4.11	Inspection and test status
4.12	Control of nonconforming product
4.13	Corrective action
4.14	Handling, storage, packaging and delivery
4.15	Quality records
4.16	Internal quality audits
4.17	Training
4.18	Statistical techniques

The first two elements on the list, "management responsibility" and "quality system" tend to be separated from the other elements as they relate to the *management* of the quality system whereas the remaining elements comprise the system itself. This is reflected in the structure of the model quality policy manual. All eighteen elements are discussed here.

The effectiveness of the quality system is determined by the controls which are put in place in respect of each element. These controls are then documented in the form of procedures. There are no set rules for the number of quality system or work procedures which must be written for each element as long as all the requirements (i.e. controls) are addressed and documented somewhere. You will find that one procedure touches on aspects of more than one element. For this reason, it is good practice to cross-refer procedures (possibly by means of a matrix) and to reference them in the quality policy manual. This is discussed in more detail in Step 5.

2.2.1 Management Responsibility

ISO 9002 identifies three key aspects of management responsibility:

- Quality policy
- Organisation
- Management review

Quality policy is detailed in the quality policy manual (Step 2 Appendix).

Organisation is split further into responsibility and authority, verification resources and personnel, management representative. The organisational structure (interrelation) of the company should be presented in the form of an organisation chart (or series of charts) within the quality policy manual. It is not necessary to state the names of the personnel on the charts which go into the quality policy manual, but their job titles should be stated and their responsibilities indicated – on the charts, in the narrative accompanying the charts, and in job descriptions.

The "management representative" should be specifically appointed as having *defined authority and responsibility for ensuring that the requirements of the standard are implemented and maintained*. This authority and responsibility should be stated on a job description and the quality policy manual should clearly indicate who the management representative is.

The management representative is often the person designated as the quality representative (see Step 1); alternatively, it may be the managing director or the chairman of the management review committee.

The requirement in respect of verification resources and personnel means that your company must decide, first of all, what sort of verification activities you plan to carry out (e.g. what inspections, audits, etc.) and then you must provide for people with sufficient qualifications and experience to undertake the work. This requirement is included here because these verification activities are a means of managing and controlling the quality system "on the ground". Those who perform audits should be independent of those performing the work. The standard does not stipulate what qualifications and experience are required for verification personnel, and you should therefore establish your own realistic criteria and make sure all the personnel you are using meet those criteria. These criteria should be detailed in procedures rather than in the quality policy manual (see 2.2.17 on Training). They are discussed further in the relevant elements such as inspection and test, auditing and training.

Management review involves an overview of the effectiveness of the quality system to make sure policies and objectives are being fulfilled and to evaluate the need for any change in policies and objectives resulting from changing circumstances. The review should take into account the results of internal audits, corrective action analyses, etc. (see Step 1).

2.2.2 Quality System

It may seem confusing for there to be a specific element in the standard on the quality system when it is the overall subject of the standard. The requirement of this element, however, is the *planning*, *documentation* and *implementation* of the system, to make sure that all other functions have been properly taken into account, e.g. customer liaison, manufacturing, purchasing, subcontracting, training and installation. You must be able to provide evidence of planning, documentation and implementation.

The quality policy manual should indicate which standard is used in the quality system and how the system is documented and implemented (see section 2.0 of the model quality policy manual in the Appendix of Step 2). Implementation of the "development schedule" described in section 3.2 of Step 4 will ensure that timely consideration is given to all of the aspects involved in developing the quality system.

2.2.3 Contract Review

The requirements of the standard can be defined as making sure that you know *exactly* what the contract, specification, order, etc., involves and making sure you are capable of carrying out the work before you agree or commit the company to do so. If the final order or contract differs from the terms set out in a tender, you must resolve and document the differences before you start work. Furthermore, you are required to have a system for these activities and you must keep records as evidence of this system. This involves preparing a contract review procedure.

This is one of the "key" elements in the quality system as the definition of "quality", which is discussed in the Introduction section of this handbook, is the continual fulfilment of contractual requirements. Therefore, it is imperative that the contract requirements are clearly defined, documented and understood by all parties of the contract. It is also important to identify and resolve any differences between the tender (where appropriate) and the final contract to ensure they are legitimate requirements, that they are costed for and can be accommodated.

It is the responsibility of your company to assess that you have the capability and resources to carry out the work, in the time scale agreed. It is pointless and commercially unviable to accept a contract which cannot be fulfilled. This assessment should be ongoing if there is any time lag between award of the contract and commencement of the work. *Liaise with your clients as much as is necessary.*

The definition of a "contract" in this context can be:

- a formal tender exercise;
- a written purchase order (e.g. for catalogue items);
- a telephone call or fax requesting goods or services.

In cases where the initial request is not followed up by documentation from your customer, e.g. a telephone call, you should record the details and send a copy to the customer by way of confirmation. This provides evidence of your understanding of the contract requirements, and it is then up to the customer to respond if there are any discrepancies.

The system for undertaking this assessment (i.e. the contract review) can be as simple as a form or a stamp which is circulated to relevant personnel for their approval, e.g. an order for a catalogue-type item or one of the company's "standard" products could be approved for capability by the sales manager, the production manager and the finance manager. The approved documents would form the record of the review. If the order is for a special product, or for an unusual quantity or perhaps for an accelerated time scale, these managers (and/or others) could be asked to detail any additional resources required or indicate the impact on other orders, again providing a record of this review.

Another alternative is the preparation of a quality plan for each major contract. This is probably more relevant to engineering and construction companies than to product manufacturers. It could also be applicable to service companies where jobs or contracts may vary.

2.2.4 Document Control

A "document" in the context of the quality system includes a whole range of examples such as specifications, instructions, standards, procedures, job descriptions, drawings, etc.

The requirements of the standard can be simply defined as ensuring that you have control over all documents which you think could affect the quality system and the quality of the product or service. The main objective is to ensure that those personnel who need certain information, data or documents to perform their duties are using only the correct issues or versions of such documents and data, as required by their particular jobs. For example, a drawing is a key document on a construction project and it is not difficult to imagine the consequence of an incorrect or superseded drawing being used unknowingly at the outset of the project! Obsolete documents must be withdrawn from use and evidence should exist that withdrawal has taken place from all locations of issue.

The requirement of ISO 9002 states the control is over *all* aspects of such documentation - preparation, review, approval, issue, referencing, filing, amending, removal and disposal. Documents and data in this context include written (hardcopy) information and information received, stored or transmitted by electronic media, i.e. computers and word processors. The obvious difficulties in approving/signing documents on a floppy disk mean that the controls have to be applied in accessing, amending and deleting such documents.

An important aspect to bear in mind is that it is up to you to specify what documents you wish to control in the first place. Not every document in the company can be considered as having a material effect on the quality system. You must therefore make a sensible judgement about which documents are important, based on the implications of the wrong information being used and the resultant effect on the quality of the company's goods or services. At the very least, however, you should have systems and procedures to control:

- the quality policy manual;
- quality system and work procedures;
- tender and contract documents;
- quality plans;
- technical and product specifications and drawings;
- national and international standards;
- statutory, legal and regulatory approvals;
- inspection and test plans.

As document control is a function which affects almost every part of the business, you will probably find it necessary to develop several procedures to cover all aspects of control and the variety of documents to be controlled. Included in the above types of document will be customer-supplied, as well as internally-generated documentation, and relevant correspondence, both incoming and outgoing.

Note: It is worthwhile highlighting the distinction between "documents", per section 4.4 of ISO 9002, and "quality records", per section 4.15. The distinction can be simply expressed as documents being used as *inputs* into the quality system and quality records forming *outputs*. For example, a drawing would be considered as a document, but the drawing register would be a quality record. ISO 9002 requires documents to be controlled but quality records only need to be properly maintained. (Quality records will be discussed later in 2.2.15.)

2.2.5 Purchasing

The standard identifies three aspects of purchasing:

- Assessment of subcontractors
- Purchasing data
- Verification of purchased product

Expressed in simple terms, the requirements in respect of these elements are as follows:

- You must only use subcontractors or suppliers (goods and services) who can demonstrate that they are consistently capable of meeting your requirements, and you must have a system for assessing their performance and suitability.
- You must clearly define your requirements in purchasing documents, i.e. the orders or contracts which you place or agree with your subcontractors. (This mirrors the requirements of section 4.3 of the standard for contracts review between you, as a supplier, and your client.) Your requirements may be contained in specifications, drawings, instructions, purchase orders, etc., and may specify what standard of quality system you wish your subcontractor to have in place.
- Your client may wish to verify or check the product or service itself, either at source (your site) or when it is received into his site. You have to agree in your contract with your client that he has the right to verify products and services in this way. You should note, however, that such verification by your client does not alter your responsibility to satisfy the contract requirements and your client still has the right to reject any unsatisfactory goods or services. In the same way, your client may wish to check out your supplier (the subcontractor), but you are still ultimately responsible for the quality of the product or service.

(*Note:* In the context of this section, your company is still referred to as the "supplier", as is the case in all the other sections of the standard. The reason for this is that you are deemed to be implementing the standard to be able to satisfy your customers' needs. Your customers are therefore the "purchasers", as in 2.2.6 later. In turn, your suppliers are referred to in the standard as "subcontractors". Therefore, read all references in the standard to "the supplier" as applying to your company.)

The practical implementation of these requirements involves the following activities and procedures:

Subcontractor assessment

- Decide which criteria you wish to use to assess your subcontractors, e.g. whether or not they have an appropriate, certified quality system in place, the number of complaints or rejections you have made over a set period, how critical certain goods and services are to your final product or service, what quality control checks you have carried out at their or your sites, their apparent capability to supply certain goods and services, or even the degree of choice you have of suppliers of some items. You should not automatically assess suppliers as being acceptable solely on the grounds that they have certified quality system (e.g. to ISO 9002), without carrying out some, or all, of the other forms of assessment.
- Establish an "approved suppliers register", or perhaps several registers for

different types of goods and services, and include suppliers who have been successfully assessed. You may wish to "rate" several suppliers for various goods and services in order of preference.

- Establish a system for continually monitoring the performance of subcontractors/suppliers, e.g. periodic checks on products, appraisal questionnaires about their quality controls and checks, logging of complaints and rejections for evaluation, make sure that unacceptable suppliers are taken off the register and that relevant personnel are informed of the fact and reasons behind it.

Purchasing data

- Develop standardised means of placing purchase orders for various types of goods and services, to ensure that you correctly specify all your requirements. For example, you may require certificates or test results in some cases, product identification in other cases, or perhaps delivery within a specified time scale. If you do not properly specify all your requirements and agree on them with your supplier, you have no basis for assessing the quality of bought-in goods and services which will ultimately affect your final product/service.
- Make sure that these purchasing documents are properly approved within your company before being transmitted to suppliers.

Verification of purchased product

- If your client believes that certain goods and services are critical or highly specialised and it is important to see them being processed at your or your supplier's site, he should provide for such inspection in the purchasing documentation/contract. You, in turn, must agree on this with your suppliers, if relevant, as you cannot assume an automatic right for your client to visit their premises. You must also be clear that your client can still reject your work and the work of your subcontractors at a later stage if necessary. (*Note:* Where work is sub-subcontracted, you should ensure that the contract documents still afford you the right of verification.)

2.2.6 Purchaser-supplied Product

In this context, the "purchaser" is your customer. Your customer may provide you with some of the goods and services which will go into the final product, commonly referred to as "free issue materials" and generally associated with, but not always, a construction contract needing the forward purchase of "long lead" items. You must view these goods and services in the same way as purchased items discussed in 2.2.5, i.e. make sure they are fit for their purpose and that you store and maintain them properly, as if they were the company's property, during all stages of the process. If any items are found to be damaged upon receipt, or incorrect for the work, or damaged, or lost whilst in your possession, you must document them and report them to your customer.

You may wish to use the same or similar procedures as for section 2.2.9, incorporating the requirement for notification of damage, loss, etc.

This section may not apply in all cases to your company but you should nevertheless reference it in your quality policy manual stating why it is inapplicable or make some provision in the event that purchaser-supplied products are applicable in the future.

2.2.7 Product Identification and Traceability

Although they are closely related, "identification" and "traceability" are separate aspects, requiring different activities to achieve compliance with the quality system standard.

Identification is the physical marking of the product or the documentation accompanying the product (e.g. job card) through the manufacturing process in such a manner that the work can be referenced to applicable documentation. The type of identification often used is the marking of the work's job number, part number or drawing number on the actual workpiece or the container in which components are kept prior to assembly but it could be in the form of a tag attached to the product, or actually stamped, painted or etched onto the product. The purpose of product identification is to ensure that products and parts for different jobs are not mixed up. Identification should be maintained at *all* stages of the process.

Traceability is a contractual requirement and is the use of identification markers through the process (say, manufacturing) so that a record is maintained of exactly which raw materials or components have been used to produce the finished product. Traceability is achieved by transferring identification markings from "parent" items to sub-items, either physically or in the accompanying documentation, maintaining a record of material location and, finally transferring the details onto the mechanical and physical test certificates if required.

Examples of identification and traceability might be: the manufacture and assembly of a custom-made car, according to a customer's specification which requires individual components and raw materials to be traceable to source and to inspection and test certificates/records. In this example, the identification could be the customer's order number, e.g. 0012/91, and this order number would then be marked on all items of materials or components designated to be used to assemble the car, or marked on tags attached to these items. The identification status must be maintained throughout production, if necessary, by transferring this number from one item which is sub-divided, or processed onto the resulting item. The traceability would be achieved by recording the details of the individual components such as the radiator, cylinders, exhaust, etc., on the documentation accompanying the car, e.g. a work's traveller card. The details recorded would include the manufacture of the component, any batch or product numbers, the results of any inspections and tests and the location of the item.

As the standard implies, identification is only required, "where appropriate", and traceability is only required when specified in contractual documentation. Most companies would have systems in place for identification of goods and materials, e.g. job numbers, stock references, batch numbers, etc. You should document such systems in the form of procedures and take into account the requirements your customers have for traceability. These requirements may differ between customers.

Identification and traceability are essential in some industries, such as pharmaceutical and food, where products may need to be recalled for health or safety reasons.

2.2.8 Process Control

Defining your company's "process" is not always as easy as it sounds, especially for service-related companies. The process can be simply stated as the core function of your company's operations which results in a defined output to meet your customer's requirements – whether the output is a product, a service or even an idea. Therefore, examples of processes might be, in a manufacturing context, the act of transforming raw materials into a finished product by fabrication, assembly or machining, or in a service context, the act of transporting goods from A to B. Every company has one or more processes and you should clearly define your company's process(es) before considering the relevant quality controls to apply.

The standard makes a distinction between processes which can be inspected and tested before the product is released for use and other processes where full inspection and testing is not possible, perhaps resulting in damage to the product. These latter processes have been classified as "special processes", e.g. welding, NDT, painting and heat treatment.

The requirements of the standard in respect of process control can be simply expressed as making sure your processes are carried out under *controlled conditions*, which is most effectively achieved by having well documented work procedures, covering every phase of manufacture, assembly and installation, and by clearly documenting and communicating the customer's specified requirements including the standards of workmanship and quality required. It is important also to take into account the proper *planning* and *co-ordination* of the processing activities, including the identification and selection of suitable personnel and equipment. This comes back to the need for quality plans (see 2.6 later) to meet differing client requirements.

Section 2.7 of the model quality policy manual covers the key aspects of process control, highlighting the links with contract review and inspection and test activities.

In the case of *special processes*, such as welding, heat treatment, non-destructive testing (NDT), etc., where the results cannot be verified by subsequent inspection, there must be procedures in place for carrying out these processes which have been evaluated and which can demonstrate that the output meets the required specification. This is normally done by periodic samples and the procedure itself is then referred to as a "qualified" procedure.

2.2.9 Inspection and Testing

The standard identifies three stages of inspection and testings:

- on incoming goods or raw materials
- during the processing or manufacturing
- on final products before they are released

The main objectives of inspection and testing activities are:

- to ensure that specified requirements (both yours and your customer's) are *conformed to* at all times;
- to ensure that *nonconforming* products, materials, etc., are identified as such so that they are either not used at all or used in the knowledge that they are "sub-standard" (and agreed as such with customers). (*Note:* To supply materials, goods or assemblies with known nonconformances, but which are acceptable to your customer, is referred to as obtaining a "concession" to supply and use "as is". A separate procedure called a "concession request" is usually developed for this eventuality.)

Inspection and testing involves activities such as measuring, sampling, checking against agreed, defined criteria. These criteria should obviously relate to the specification for the goods or services, and they should be documented in the procedures so that the inspection and testing is done on a consistent basis.

We have made reference to inspection and test plans (ITPs) in section 2.8 of the model quality policy manual and an example of an ITP form is shown in Figure 4. These may not be necessary for every company and will probably depend on the extent to which your customer specifies essential inspection and test results. The purpose of the ITP is to provide confirmation of conformance of specific activities in a contract or job. The activity column should list all significant stages of manufacture, process or service activity, *in chronological order*, against the specific item of equipment or service. The type of check or inspection will be determined by the contract or applicable code/standard, e.g. measurement, or checking

INSPECTION AND TEST PLAN

Project: ______________________

Item: ______________________ Contractor: ______________________

Ref: ______________________ Subcontractor: ______________________

ACTIVITY	CHECK AND INSPECTIONS	APPLICABLE STANDARD	ACCEPTANCE CRITERIA	INSPECTORATE			REMARKS
				SUB-CONT.	CONT.	CLIENT OR C/A	

C denotes certification required * denotes inspection H denotes hold point

Figure 4 An Inspection and Test Plan form

certification. The applicable standard could be the specification, material codes, statutory requirements, etc., and the acceptance criteria will state the upper and lower limits of acceptability of tolerance. The inspectorate column gives options on nominating the level of inspection for any activity, e.g. third party, or client.

Although the objectives of inspection and testing are the same in each of the three stages referred to here, the activities are different and you will probably find that separate procedures will be most effective. It is important, also, that the personnel you appoint to carry out the inspection and test activities are suitably qualified or experienced to do so (see also 2.2.1 and 2.2.17).

2.2.10 Inspection, Measuring and Test Equipment

Despite the lengthy wording of this element of the standard, the intent is quite simple, i.e. to provide you and your customer with a high level of confidence that the equipment you use to inspect, measure and test (per section 2.9 of the model quality policy manual) is suitable and capable of performing its required functions. The equipment concerned can range from items such as pressure gauges, jigs, micrometers, etc., to quite sophisticated electronic monitoring devices. The key requirements of this element are:

- that you identify all such equipment, whether you own it or hire it from a specialist firm;
- that you calibrate such equipment, or ensure it is calibrated, and adjusted in accordance with defined procedures and accepted criteria as recommended by the equipment supplier or relevant (including national) standards on calibration criteria;
- that you keep records of calibrations and adjustments carried out (e.g. a log book) and that you also show the calibration status on the equipment itself (e.g. a tag giving next due calibration date);
- that you undertake calibrations, inspections, tests, etc., in suitable conditions, ensuring the equipment is handled and stored properly.

The extent to which this element applies to your company will depend on the nature of your business. For example, if it is difficult to undertake tests on the final product itself (see 2.2.8), it may be more important to have confidence in the inspections and tests carried out during the process. This also applies to products where the technical specification is very rigid and it is extremely costly to rework certain processes, e.g. communications equipment.

On the other hand, some companies may have simple, unsophisticated inspection and test equipment such as rulers, or perhaps no such equipment at all in the case of some service industries.

2.2.11 Inspection and Test Status

Irrespective of the number and types of inspections and tests carried out, it is important to identify which products or items have actually been inspected/tested so that everyone knows whether they are conforming or nonconforming (see 2.2.9). This can be as simple as a mark or stamp on the item, or a tag attached to it, or a work's traveller, but it should stay with the item as it moves through the production process.

You should also define who is authorised to decide whether a product is acceptable, or "conforming". Items which have not passed inspection should be clearly marked as such (see 2.2.12 of this section).

2.2.12 Control of Nonconforming Products

The requirement of the standard is two-fold:

- that you record, identify and segregate (if possible) nonconforming products;
- that you have a defined procedure for deciding what to do with it, e.g. repair, rework, scrap, downgrade, or apply for a concession from your customer to accept it "as is" (see 2.2.9).

Nonconforming products are those which "fail" the various inspections and tests which you carry out, as discussed in the preceding paragraphs. The reasons for undertaking these inspections and tests and for identifying the test status of products now become clear, as you take out of the process those products which do not meet your "quality" criteria. You may not always be able to physically segregate such products but they must be clearly identified and prevented from being used until you have decided what to do with them. Ideally, you should establish one or more "quarantine" areas, as appropriate.

Identifying products as nonconforming does not mean that they are useless altogether as it may be possible to modify them or use them for a different purpose or perhaps apply to your customer for a concession, as long as the customer agrees to it. You should define who has the authority to decide on what to do with nonconforming product and the decision should be made in accordance with a procedure for review and recording of the decision taken. This record is a key aspect of the quality system, enabling analysis of nonconformances and development of corrective actions.

2.2.13 Corrective Action

This is another key element in determining the effectiveness of the quality system: i.e. not only should the system be able to prevent nonconforming products being used in the process but it should provide a mechanism for making sure that the reasons and factors causing the nonconformances are identified and that action is taken to prevent their recurrence. Generally, control of nonconforming products (2.2.12 of this section) relates to the *product or service* itself, whereas in this section, corrective action also relates to *system* deficiencies. The system is therefore made effective by reducing the occurrence of nonconformances.

To be able to take corrective action you need to have a properly defined system for identifying and reviewing the nonconformances, whether they have arisen from incorrect working methods, failure to conform to procedures, defective specifications or any other source including subcontracted work. This means keeping records of nonconformances, including the decision on their disposal, re-work, etc., which can be analysed to identify causes. For example, a log of customer complaints could be maintained for analysis of the types of complaints, and a register could be kept of rejected material or products during the production process indicating why rejection was necessary. Internal audit reports (see 2.2.16) are another source of identifying nonconformances, e.g. noncompliance with procedures, which may result in procedures being amended if they are unworkable.

You should designate authority for reviewing such reports and records and for recommending the necessary corrective actions. The implementation of the corrective actions should be the responsibility of senior management and they should also consider the results of the analysis of the cause of nonconformances, at their management review meetings (see 2.2.1), in order to identify any trends for correction.

2.2.14 Handling, Storage, Packaging and Delivery

The requirements of this element apply not only to finished products but also to raw materials, components, and work-in-progress. The requirement is quite simply that you have proper methods and procedures to maintain the quality of such items, avoiding damage or deterioration, until they cease to become your responsibility. "Maintaining the quality" in this context is not just the physical state of the product but also aspects such as identification status (e.g. markings on packaging) and the segregation of products where appropriate, to avoid confusion or misuse.

In order to define your handling, storage, packaging and delivery procedures you should, first of all, establish any specialised needs for particular products or materials, e.g. for delicate items or items which might deteriorate quickly, such as foodstuffs. Obviously, you should then ensure that you have the capability to meet these requirements – you should already have done this anyway at the contract review stage (see 2.2.3 of this section).

Written procedures should govern the way a product is handled and protected during processing, and should ensure that a special product is not mixed with a similar product of unknown or dissimilar quality (e.g. paints, fuels, fluids), that there is no contamination, that delicate parts are protected and that a product does not miss any operation or inspection, etc.

Delivery of a product often forms part of the contractual requirements and the responsibility for the quality of the product is not passed on until it reaches its final destination. In this type of situation, delivery and handling methods are just as important in maintaining quality as all of the other processing methods involved in producing the product itself.

2.2.15 Quality Records

As discussed in 2.2.4, quality records can be viewed as the documentary *outputs* from the system, providing the objective evidence that the quality system is effective in meeting customers' requirements. Such quality records will arise from a variety of sources, including subcontractors and your customers. Examples of quality records are:

- contract review notes;
- inspection and test reports;
- material and test certificates;
- audit reports;
- management review records.

The requirements of this element are simply for these records to be properly assembled and maintained and to be easily identified and accessed, for both internal and external purposes.

You should develop procedures describing what records you intend to maintain, how they should be referenced and filed, where they should be stored and how long they should be kept. The retention times may vary for different types of records and will depend on your type of business and any periods you agree with your customers. You should state the retention times for each type of record in writing and you should also clearly define who has the authority to dispose of quality records.

2.2.16 Internal Quality Audits

The concept of internal quality audits is much the same as financial audits which you may be more familiar with. The techniques are the same: the operations are examined and assessed against defined criteria (whether they are standard accounting practices or your quality system procedures) using checklists and sampling techniques, and resulting in a report highlighting errors and deficiencies.

Internal quality audits are very important in determining the overall effectiveness of the quality system: they complement the more specific assessments and reviews such as nonconformance and corrective action. In turn, management makes use of the results of internal quality audits in management reviews. The internal quality audits will probe the way personnel operate and will check to see that procedures are being adhered to. They will also examine your documentation and quality records to check these are being controlled and maintained correctly.

Step 6 of this handbook gives more detailed guidelines on internal quality audits. You should document procedures for auditing, develop regular audit schedules to cover all aspects of the quality system, and establish a mechanism for reporting and implementing corrective actions arising from the audits.

2.2.17 Training

Training, education and quality awareness are covered in more detail in Step 4 of this handbook. The requirements of the standard are four-fold:

- You should establish the training *needs* of personnel in relation to their jobs, e.g. specific "on-the-job" training and supervision in new techniques or working methods.
- You should provide training to meet these needs.
- You should identify the necessary qualifications and experience for individual jobs and make sure that the job holders meet these requirements.
- You should keep records of qualifications and training (in-house and external) undergone by all personnel.

The training needs of personnel can also be expanded to include a need to understand what the quality system is and how it should be made to work by means of the quality policy manual, procedures, etc., i.e. "quality awareness" training. In addition to the activities described in Step 3, this can be achieved through internal induction programs and seminars, or through appropriate external courses.

The need for training to make the quality system work can be reiterated as *"the quality of your output is only as good as the quality of your input"*. *Input* is not just materials, goods and documentation; it is also the skills, experience, knowledge, motivation and commitment of your personnel.

2.2.18 Statistical Techniques

The need for statistical techniques will depend on the type of operation or business your company is in. Statistical techniques involve methods of sampling data or products for examination, determining acceptance criteria, classifying product characteristics and variance/regression analyses, as well as a number of other techniques. Statistical techniques can be used to make best use of available data, to verify process capability and control, to analyse the causes of defects and problems and to measure or assess quality. You should therefore give careful consideration to which statistical techniques you can use to assist in making the quality system most effective.

The types of statistical technique described earlier can be derived from well-known, published techniques and you should aim to use recognisable methods as much as possible. You should document, in procedures, the statistical techniques you will use and how the results will be assessed.

2.3 PURPOSE OF THE QUALITY POLICY MANUAL

The definition of a quality policy manual is generally accepted as a document setting out the general quality policies, procedures and practices of an organisation.

The quality policy manual comprises the uppermost level or tier of quality system documentation. The pyramid chart "Quality System Documentation" in Figure 5 illustrates the hierarchy.

The purpose of the quality policy manual is to provide a formal statement of a company's quality policies and objectives and how it plans to achieve such objectives. Making a formal statement reinforces management's commitment to quality and this commitment can be directed internally, to motivate staff, and externally, to promote the company's image. The quality policy manual really defines the basis of the quality system and all the controls, processes and lower levels of documentation flow down from the objectives stated in the quality policy manual.

If you are planning to seek certification, the quality policy manual will be required for a detailed review by the assessors (this is referred to as a "desk top"

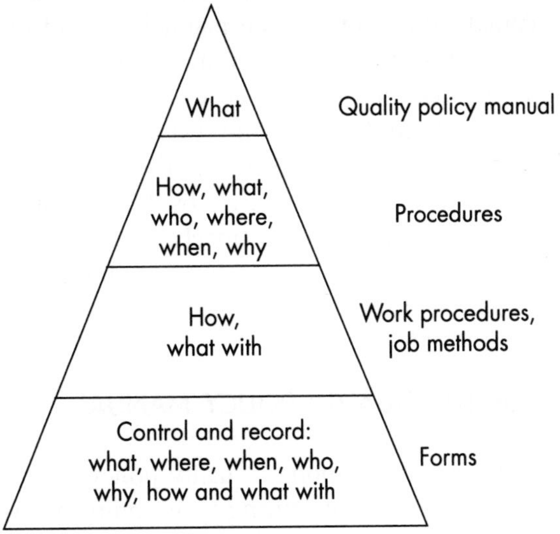
What
Quality policy manual
How, what, who, where, when, why
Procedures
How, what with
Work procedures, job methods
Control and record: what, where, when, who, why, how and what with
Forms

Figure 5 Quality system documentation

audit), some 2–3 months before the final assessment (see Step 7). You may also be required or have a desire to show your quality policy manual to clients undertaking their own supplier assessment activities. Similarly, you may wish to use your quality policy manual as a way of setting out the quality objectives which you expect *your* suppliers to meet.

2.4 CONTENTS OF THE QUALITY POLICY MANUAL

The quality policy manual should be structured in such a way that it addresses *all* of the elements and requirements of the relevant standard. Therefore, even elements which may not necessarily apply to your company (e.g. perhaps your client does not provide any free issue materials) should be referenced and the reasons for their non-applicability should be stated. It should be stressed here, however, that the majority of the system elements will apply to every company and you must read the wording of the standard *very carefully* to relate it to your own company. This is discussed in considerable depth in the following sections but the point being made is that the wording of the standard is generic and you cannot merely ignore elements because they are not immediately obvious to your company's operations.

In addition to addressing the individual "elements" of the quality system, the quality policy manual should include the quality policy statement, it should clearly define the various responsibilities for quality within the organisation (including an organisation chart) and it should define the mechanism for updating and issuing the quality policy manual. Ideally, the procedures associated with the quality policy manual should be referenced at the end.

The model quality policy manual contains guidelines on how to update and issue revisions to the manual. You should use your discretion to decide whether to re-issue the whole manual, or sections of the manual, instead of individual pages, bearing in mind the administration involved in replacing individual pages and recording the revisions, against the time and cost of re-issuing the whole manual if it is quite large. You may wish to "save up" the revisions, if they are minor, until it is worthwhile revising the whole manual. You can also highlight changes from one version to the next in a variety of ways, e.g., by highlighting (mechanically or electronically) or by drawing revision boxes (mechanically or electronically) at the side of the page alongside the revision, preferably containing the revision number. At the *next* revision, however, the previous revision indicators should be removed.

2.5 PREPARATION OF THE QUALITY POLICY MANUAL

The Appendix to Step 2 contains a "model" quality policy manual which we have put together for a hypothetical manufacturing-type company: ABC Company Pty Ltd. The purpose of including this model document in this package is to show the sort of structure, terminology and level of detail which you may wish to adopt. It must be stressed that this is *not* a universal quality policy manual and you cannot simply substitute your company's name for our hypothetical one. *You must document what you* ***actually*** *do, rather than what you would like to do*!

The other reason for including this model quality policy manual is to assist in our explanation of how to interpret the requirements of the standard and relate them to various situations. We have tried to give as much practical guidance as possible in understanding the standard and the model quality policy manual can be used in conjunction with the guidelines. (Step 5 also includes some model procedures, which are referenced at the back of the model quality policy manual.)

During the preparation of your quality policy manual you should circulate drafts of each section to relevant personnel to make sure that the company's quality objectives are agreed by all concerned and that you are documenting your actual operations. Undoubtedly you will revise your quality policy manual from time to time to reflect organisational or operational changes and you should therefore *avoid the trap of trying to allow for all possible eventualities during the life of the company.*

2.6 QUALITY PLANS

The definition of a quality plan is:

> A document setting out the specific quality practices, resources and sequence of activities relevant to a particular product, service, contract or project (ISO 8402).

The difference between a quality plan and a quality policy manual is that you may have several quality plans, for various projects or contracts, but you will only have one quality policy manual for the company as a whole. Not all companies need to develop quality plans – it depends on whether the scope of work between one contract and another varies significantly enough for separate systems, procedures and tests to be developed and documented. It also depends on whether your customer or client requires you to have a unique quality plan for a certain contract or project.

For example, an engineering company working on several construction projects for different customers or clients might prepare a quality plan for each project as the contract requirements might be quite different between projects. On the other hand, a manufacturing company may be able to encompass all of its quality policies, objectives and practices in a single document for the whole company, i.e. the quality policy manual, even although it is manufacturing a variety of products.

The guidelines included in this section for the development of the quality policy manual are also relevant to quality plans.

STEP 2

QUALITY SYSTEM REQUIREMENTS AND THE QUALITY POLICY MANUAL

Appendix Model Quality Policy Manual

ABC COMPANY PTY LTD

123 Iso Street
Widgitsville

QUALITY POLICY MANUAL

ISSUE: A DATE: XX/YY/ZZ

AUTHORISED: ______________________________

(MANAGING DIRECTOR)

CONTROLLED: ☐* COPY NUMBER: ☐

UNCONTROLLED: ☐*

(* cross as applicable)

CONTENTS

The quality policy manual, quality system procedures, and work procedures remain the sole property of ABC Co.

The customer has agreed to protect the confidentiality of all information viewed or received from ABC Co. regardless of its nature or content.

Recipients of ABC Co. documents should not copy, divulge, or distribute any documentation either within their organisation or to external third parties without prior advice to and written permission from the managing director of ABC Co.

Issue no.	Modifications	Date	Authority
A	Approved for release		[Managing director or nominated authority to sign]

Section	Page no.	Rev. no.	Amendments	Date	Authorised by
A	All	0	Issued	Nov 1992	[Signed]

Note: All pages shall revert to revision 0 upon complete re-issue of the manual.

ABC Co. manufactures in three separate production facilities which include small widgets for the domestic market and two types of wongles.

All production is propriety items which have been designed by ABC Co., Lapasia who remain the authority for approving any proposed design changes. Design is therefore not currently a consideration at ABC Co.

In addition to the implementation of quality management, ABC Co. has developed a number of technical standards which have been targeted to comply with international product standards, e.g. JSI, ASIM, etc.

This quality policy manual therefore addresses all the management and control systems for a production environment.

(*Note:* This section is used to briefly describe a company, its products, history and general scope of operations. This section must be specific to the company.)

1.0 COMPANY POLICY

1.1 QUALITY POLICY STATEMENT

ABC Co. recognises the value of customer satisfaction in a competitive world and the major contribution to this satisfaction is made by the supply of products to an assured level of quality.

To achieve this objective, the management of ABC Co. has committed itself to a quality assurance system based on the requirements of international standard ISO 9002.

The quality and reliability of our products are the responsibility of all employees. To this end, procedures covering all aspects of areas affecting quality will be developed and adhered to at all times. Provision will be made for any quality problems arising to be solved with speed and in a manner to prevent recurrence.

The procedures used in the programme are to be kept continually under review and techniques improved whenever and wherever necessary. A philosophy of continuous improvement will be adopted by ABC Co. so that the quality system will be a continuously evolving programme.

The attainment of these quality goals requires strong and responsive management and a united commitment from all staff. The outcome will be a respected reputation for the quality of our products and a rewarding place to work.

Education and training to understand company policy will be achieved through induction and structured training programmes.

____

[Name]
Managing Director

1.2 DISTRIBUTION, REVISION AND RE-ISSUE

1.2.1 Distribution

Distribution of this manual within the company and to our third party certification body is on a controlled copy basis. Distribution of controlled copies is at the discretion of the managing director. A list of copy holders are kept by the document control.

Controlled copies are subject to revision servicing and are marked:

Copy no.: .....
Controlled: (X)

Where requested and approved by the quality manager, copies of the manual will be provided to customers to meet contractual obligations or for other purposes. Unless specifically requested, these copies will not be subject to revision servicing and are marked:

Uncontrolled: (X)

1.2.2 Revision

Revisions to the manual are made as required to accurately reflect the current organisation and quality practices of the company. Revisions are made by replacement of the applicable page(s). Each revised page is identified by a revision number and date of revision. The revised text is identified by *underlining the section where a revision has occurred.*

Revisions are numbered consecutively until such time as a new issue is produced which incorporates all changes. When changes affect a considerable number of pages, the manual will be re-issued as a new issue. Issues are identified by letters in alphabetical order. Each issue cancels and replaces all previous issues and revisions.

The revisions list indicates all the revisions to the latest issue of the manual.

1.2.3 Re-issue

The manual will be issued automatically to all holders of controlled copies. It is the responsibility of the copy holders to update their copies and destroy obsolete copies.

1.3 ORGANISATION

1.3.1 General

An organisation chart (see Figure 6) shows the various departments, functions and reporting relationships within the company. *In the absence of any individual within the company, responsibility is delegated to the next available officer down in the organisation chart.*

Full job descriptions for all categories of ABC Co. personnel are retained by the managing director and define personnel responsibilities and authorities for:

(a) initiating action to prevent the occurrence of product nonconformity and quality system noncompliance;
(b) identifying and recording product quality problems;
(c) initiating, recommending and providing solutions through designated channels;
(d) verifying the implementation of solutions;
(e) controlling further processing, delivery or installation of nonconforming product until the deficiency or unsatisfactory condition has been corrected.

1.3.2 Responsibility and Authority – Managing Director

The managing director is the executive responsible for quality and for ensuring that the quality policy statement is implemented, understood and maintained at all levels in the organisation. In this respect, the policy statement is a stand-alone document exhibited throughout the company on corporate letterhead. The managing director shall appoint a management representative for quality.

1.3.3 Responsibility and Authority – Quality Manager

1.3.3.1 Authority

The quality manager is the final authority on all matters relating to quality and quality policy throughout the company's operation. He is directly responsible to the managing director, and is the ABC Co.'s management representative for ensuring that all the requirements outlined in this manual are effectively implemented and maintained.

1.3.3.2 Responsibilities

The quality manager has the prime responsibility to develop and maintain the quality system to ensure compliance with quality requirements.

The quality manager is responsible for, but not limited to the following activities:

(a) Maintaining quality system documentation.
(b) Reviewing the organisational relationships as they affect quality and developing proposals for improvement.
(c) Monitoring ABC Co.'s quality system to determine compliance with the requirements of ISO 9002.
(d) Developing and maintaining the company's quality training programme.
(e) Resolving all matters associated with quality in the company.
(f) Monitoring the ABC Co.'s quality system by means of auditing, to determine:
- that quality policies are being adhered to;
- where improvements are needed;
- verifying implementation of the necessary corrective action.

(g) Liaising with customers' quality assurance representatives (QAR), to ensure that actual or potential quality problems are resolved.

1.3.4 Responsibility and Authority – Production Manager

With regard to quality, the production manager is responsible for:

(a) the quality of work carried out by personnel within their respective areas;
(b) verifying that approved procedures are adopted, and any necessary complementary procedures are prepared, updated and implemented.

(*Note:* Extend this section to include the quality responsibilities of all managers to include training, decision making, etc.)

1.3.5 Resources and Personnel

The managing director is responsible for identifying overall requirements for personnel and equipment to ensure effective management and performance of work.

The quality manager is responsible for identifying verification requirements and providing adequate resources in the quality system for inspection, testing and monitoring of the company's manufacturing activity and for auditing the quality system.

All personnel assigned to verification activities are suitably trained and/or qualified for their assigned tasks. Auditing personnel will be independent of those having direct responsibility for the work being performed.

1.3.6 Management Review

Management review consists of the managing director, quality manager, production manager and purchasing manager who periodically, but not less than twice per year, review the effectiveness and suitability of the quality system. Records of the review meetings are documented and maintained.

The reviews take into account data from the following system activities and/or feedback:

(a) Internal quality audit reports
(b) External audit reports
(c) Customer complaints
(d) Employee feedback
(e) Outstanding corrective action
(f) Training needs
(g) Suppliers

Further specific details are defined in procedure QP.02.

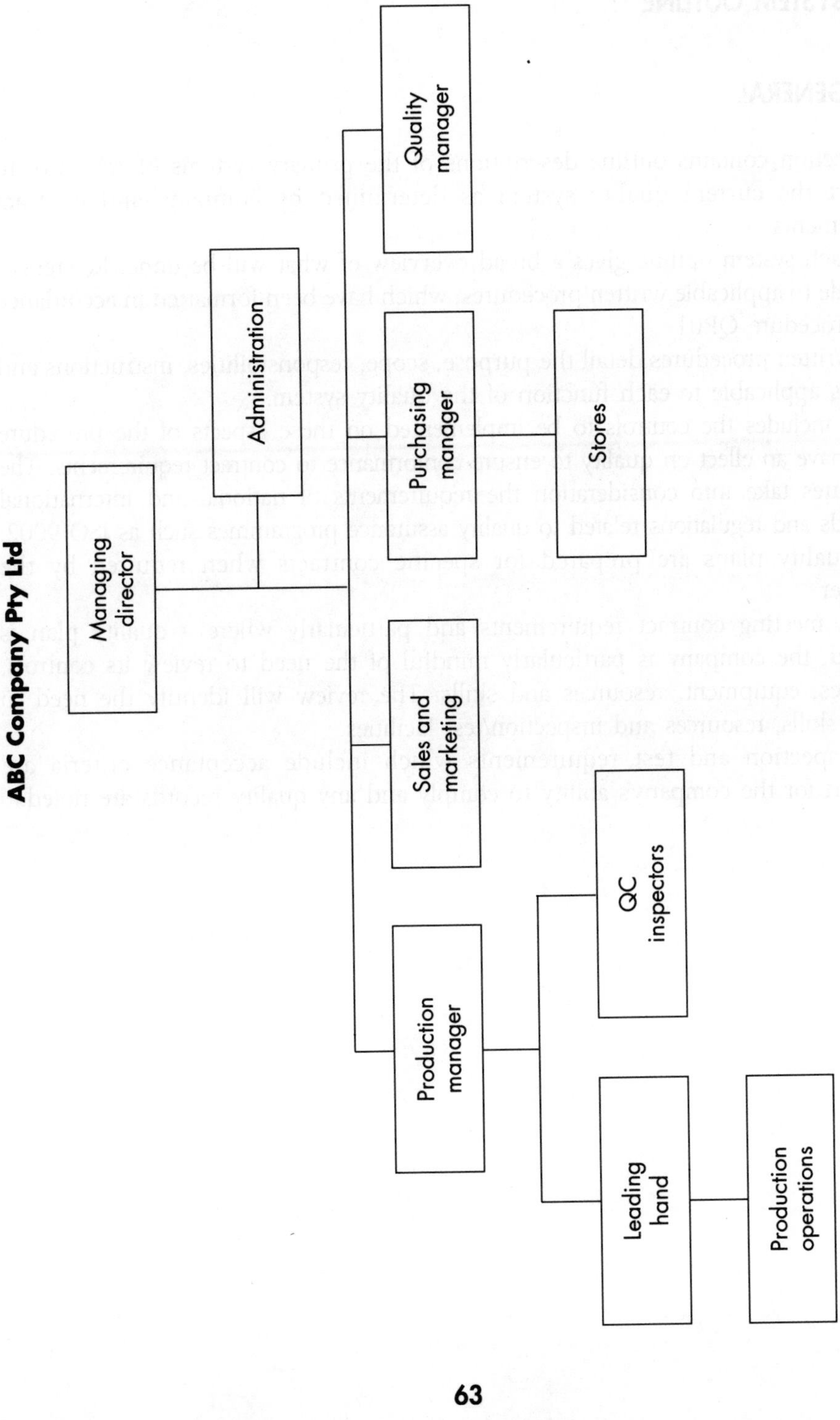
ABC Company Pty Ltd
Managing director
Administration
Quality manager
Purchasing manager
Stores
Sales and marketing
Production manager
QC inspectors
Leading hand
Production operations

Figure 6 Organisation chart

2.0 SYSTEM OUTLINE

2.1 GENERAL

This section contains outline descriptions of the primary systems of ABC Co. to support the current quality system as determined by company and contract requirements.

Each system outline gives a broad overview of what will be done. References are made to applicable written procedures, which have been formatted in accordance with procedure QP.01.

Written procedures detail the purpose, scope, responsibilities, instructions and controls applicable to each function of the quality system.

It includes the controls to be implemented on those aspects of the procedure which have an effect on quality to ensure conformance to contract requirements. The procedures take into consideration the requirements of national and international standards and regulations related to quality assurance programmes such as ISO 9002.

Quality plans are prepared for specific contracts when required by the customer.

In meeting contract requirements and particularly where a quality plan is required, the company is particularly mindful of the need to review its controls, processes, equipment, resources and skills. The review will identify the need to update skills, resources and inspection/test facilities.

Inspection and test requirements which include acceptance criteria are reviewed for the company's ability to comply and any quality records are noted.

2.2 CONTRACT REVIEW

2.2.1 System Outline

Tender and contract documentation (e.g. enquiries, tenders, bids, offers, purchase orders) are reviewed at the earliest opportunity, and in any event, prior to the work commencing.

The purpose of the review is to ensure the following:

(a) The requirements of the contract are adequately defined, understood and documented.
(b) Prior to bidding for, or accepting a contract, all requirements of the customer's specification can be complied with.
(c) Any problems associated with complying with the customer's requirements are identified and resolved.
(d) Necessary resources, facilities and personnel will be available at the required time.
(e) The requirements of a contract and the terms of the order are the same as those on which the tender was based, and any which are not are resolved.
(f) The planning of work is established and initiated after acceptance of the contract.

2.2.2 Tender Review

Prior to tender submission all relevant codes, standards, statutory requirements and customer's requirements are identified, and ABC Co.'s ability to comply, are confirmed.

Other items reviewed include availability of key personnel, resources, materials, commercial conditions, quality plan requirements, specialised training and equipment.

Actual or potential difficulties associated with any of the above are documented and resolved with the customer.

2.2.3 Contract Review

Upon receipt of customer's order, the following actions are taken:

(a) Scope of work contained in the order is compared with the tender documentation and any variations noted.
(b) Availability of key personnel and facilities is confirmed.
(c) Commercial conditions (including costing) of the contract are compared

against those in the tender and any variations noted.

(d) All aspects of the customer's requirements are reviewed.

If necessary, a meeting is held with the customer to resolve any differences prior to accepting an order.

Records are kept of all tender and contract reviews and form part of the job file.

Further specific details are identified in procedure QP.03.

2.3 DOCUMENT CONTROL

2.3.1 System Outline

All documents, drawings and data which affect quality (either internally produced or customer supplied) and which are essential to the completion of work are systematically controlled and maintained in order to ensure that the pertinent issue is available at all points of use. Obsolete documents are promptly removed from all points of use or clearly marked as superseded.

The system of control is based on the review, approval, issue, and maintenance of documentation as either quality system documentation or customer order documentation.

2.3.2 Approval Issue and Changes

Documentation affecting quality are reviewed, approved, and authorised for adequacy by authorised personnel prior to issue. Changes to documents are reviewed and approved by the same functions that performed the original review and approval. Documents are issued and maintained, identifying the nature of the change wherever practicable. The designated authorised personnel will have access to pertinent background information prior to instigating a change.

2.3.3 Copy Control

All documents which affect quality are issued on a "controlled" or "uncontrolled" basis. Holders of controlled copies are automatically issued with updated versions. Uncontrolled copies are for information purposes only, and are not normally updated.

Holders of controlled copies may destroy or return the obsolete version to the sender on receipt of an update.

A master list of the current revision and issue of documents is maintained in order to preclude the use of non-applicable documents and to identify obsolete documents which require retention for commercial, legal or historical reasons.

All documents are re-issued after a practical number of changes.

Specific details are identified in procedure QP.04.

2.4 DESIGN CONTROL

Design control is outside the scope of this standard and is not included in ABC Company's quality system.

2.5 PURCHASING

2.5.1 System Outline

All purchases of materials, parts, and services from external suppliers and subcontractors are controlled. The system ensures that all purchases comply with specified requirements.

2.5.2 Subcontractors and Suppliers

All subcontractors and suppliers are evaluated on their ability to meet company requirements prior to engagement. Only evaluated and approved subcontractors are used by the company. Evaluation, initial and ongoing, may take the form of:

(a) assessment of the subcontractor's quality system;
(b) third party certification;
(c) incoming or inprocess inspection;
(d) records of previously demonstrated capability;
(e) references.

Suitable records detailing the evidence of evaluation are retained. Records are maintained as verification of the effectiveness of the subcontractor's quality system controls.

A register of approved subcontractors is maintained.

Ultimately, supplier selection and the type of control exercised are dependent on the type of product and past history (experience) with the company.

2.5.3 Purchasing Data

All purchase orders raised will clearly describe the product or service ordered.

All applicable requirements are included or referenced in all purchase orders. This may include details such as the precise identification of the item, relevant standards and specifications, material test certificates, inspection instructions, or the title, number and issue of the quality system international standard to be applied to the product. These requirements may include, when appropriate, supplementary requirements which are a customer's requirement of a contract placed onto ABC Co.

Purchase documents are reviewed and approved by authorised personnel prior to issue to a subcontractor/supplier.

2.5.4 Verification of Purchased Goods

When the customer reserves the right to verify at the source, or after receipt, that purchased goods conform to contract requirements, such rights are included on purchase orders to the subcontractor.

The customer's verification does not relieve ABC Co. of their responsibilities and ABC Co.'s activities shall not be influenced by the customer's verifications.

Further specific details are identified in procedure QP.05.

2.6 PURCHASER-SUPPLIED PRODUCT

2.6.1 System Outline

ABC Co. considers "purchaser-supplied product" to include any free issue material, service or equipment supplied by a customer, for incorporation into ABC Co.'s manufacturing activities and delivered back to the customer.

Purchaser-supplied products are inspected upon receipt for transit damage, quantity, type, identification, correctness and completeness of accompanying documentation.

Any product which is lost, damaged, or is otherwise unsuitable for use, either as a result of delivery or subsequent storage, is recorded and reported to the customer for verification and determination of future action.

A product which is satisfactory is appropriately identified, stored and maintained to prevent unauthorised use, improper disposal or deterioration whilst in custody.

Further specific details are identified in procedure QP.06.

2.7 PRODUCT IDENTIFICATION AND TRACEABILITY

2.7.1 System Outline

All job related records, materials, purchaser-supplied product, and associated documentation are identified with a unique job number.

2.7.2 Manufactured Goods

Manufactured goods are positively identified by means of tags or labels, highlighting customer identification, ABC Co.'s job number or other identification as appropriate.

Where it is a contract requirement, the customer and/or ABC Co.'s job number, or other identification as applicable, is cross referenced on all related documentation to ensure that efficient traceability, to the extent specified, is maintained.

2.7.3 Purchased Material

All incoming material is inspected on receipt to ensure it is properly identified to the accompanying documentation.

When traceability is a requirement of the contract or by company procedures, the items are recorded on all documents as applicable.

Further specific details are identified in procedure QP.07.

2.8 PROCESS CONTROL

2.8.1 System Outline

Operations which have a direct effect on the quality of the company's process activities are identified, planned and carried out under controlled conditions.

Documented work procedures defining the manner of control, use of suitable materials and equipment and compliance with standards or quality plans are used. Documented work procedures are approved by the production manager indicating approval of the procedure and equipment to be used for control of the process.

Activities which directly affect the quality of the company's process activities are continually monitored by the production manager. Processes are statistically monitored by the quality manager.

2.8.2 Work Procedures

Documented work procedures are provided for use by personnel in appropriate locations, detailing inspections, tests, analysis, equipment, working environment, compliance with reference standards and codes, or demonstrations performed in accordance with requirements.

Work procedures are prepared according to a standard format for ease of reference and verification and include, where appropriate, criteria for workmanship.

The method of process control is reviewed on a regular basis.

2.8.3 Control of Special Processes

The following list identifies the special processes carried out by ABC Co.:

(a) Welding
(b) Painting
(c) [Add as necessary, e.g. heat treatment, soldering, etc.]

Special processes are performed by trained personnel using approved written procedures and controlled equipment.

Qualification results for special processes are made available for verification by the customer's representative as required.

Objective evidence in the form of quality records are generated and maintained to demonstrate compliance with contract requirements, and to the company's quality system.

Further specific details are identified in procedure QP.08.

2.9 INSPECTION AND TESTING

2.9.1 System Outline

The company's operations are monitored throughout and at the completion of work to ensure they conform to the customer's, statutory and company requirements.

An incoming product is not used or processed until it has been inspected and accepted as conforming to specified requirements.

2.9.2 Receiving Inspection and Testing

All goods supplied in accordance with a purchase order are inspected upon receipt for transit damage, quantity, type, identification, correctness and completeness of accompanying documentation and compliance with the purchase order. Uninspected goods are only released for urgent production purposes under positive recall conditions.

2.9.3 In-process Inspection and Testing

All work is subject to inspections and tests at appropriately defined stages of production, as controlled by work procedures and inspection and test plans. Where specified, products are held until the required inspections and tests are complete and the necessary records have been verified. A nonconforming product is suitably identified.

2.9.4 Final Inspection and Testing

Completed goods are inspected and tested in accordance with the requirements of work procedures, job cards and/or inspection and test plans as applicable.

Records and reports are examined to verify the following:

(a) All in-process inspections, tests and procedures have been satisfactorily completed.
(b) Records have been completed and signed and dated by the relevant personnel.
(c) Any special customer nominated inspections, tests or procedures have been completed and documented.
(d) The completed item has the required appearance, identification, content, and meets customer's requirements.
(e) Nonconforming items have been processed in accordance with appropriate procedures.

(f) All data complies with contract requirements.

2.9.5 Inspection and Test Records

Records of all inspections and tests (which give evidence that the product has met defined acceptance criteria) are maintained in the job file as defined in section 2.15 of this manual.

Further specific details are identified in procedure QP.09A and OP.09B.

2.10 INSPECTION, MEASURING AND TEST EQUIPMENT

2.10.1 System Outline

All inspection, measuring and test equipment, whether owned by the company, or private individuals, are controlled and calibrated to demonstrate conformance of product with specified requirements.

2.10.2 Control of Inspection, Measuring and Test Equipment

All inspection, measuring and test equipment are selected, used, and calibrated with full knowledge of the accuracy (uncertainty), capability, range, stability, and environmental conditions of use.

All equipment is identified with a unique equipment number which is traceable to appropriate records defining equipment type, location and frequency of checks.

Inspection, measuring and testing equipment design documents and/or manufacturer's brochures of the equipment are available to the customer's representative and other authorised personnel to demonstrate the adequacy and accuracy of the equipment.

All equipment is stored and handled in a manner to prevent deterioration, damage, or alteration to the functional or dimensional characteristics.

2.10.3 Calibration of Equipment

All measuring and test equipment and devices used (including privately owned) are calibrated in accordance with an established calibration and maintenance schedule and associated work procedures which detail check methods, acceptance criteria and action required when results are unsatisfactory.

All inspection, measuring and test equipment have a tag, sticker or other suitable means to indicate the equipment number and calibration status. Where this is not practical, calibration status is traceable through the calibration record card.

The identity of all inspection, measuring and test equipment (utilised for specific tests, measurements and inspections) is recorded in the job file for each job.

Measuring devices are calibrated using certified equipment which is traceable to nationally and/or internationally recognised standards.

Where equipment is found to require adjustment or recalibration, then previous activities from that equipment are assessed for validity. This assessment is documented.

Inspection, measuring and test equipment are not used if the calibration life has expired.

Suitable records of calibration are maintained. Calibration records are periodically evaluated to ascertain the adequacy of calibration intervals.

2.10.4 Test Hardware and Software

Where test hardware (such as jigs and templates) and test software are used for inspection purposes, they will meet the requirements of policies mentioned above.

Hardware and software are checked to prove they are capable of verifying product acceptability prior to being used in production.

Specific details are identified in procedure QP.10.

2.11 INSPECTION AND TEST STATUS

2.11.1 System Outline

Inspected incoming materials and production work are marked with suitable indicators or are directed to specific locations which identify the status of inspection and/or test.

2.11.2 Status

The system of indicating inspection status adequately identifies items which are:

(a) uninspected;
(b) inspected and rejected;
(c) inspected and accepted.

Nonconforming items are segregated from conforming items or suitably marked to indicate nonconformance.

The production manager and leading hands are the authorities responsible for releasing any conforming product. This will be shown on release records.

Inspection and test status of incoming purchased products will be indicated by signing of the purchase order after receipt of the material. Production inspection and test status ensures that only product that has passed the required inspection and test is released for further work.

2.12 CONTROL OF NONCONFORMING PRODUCT

2.12.1 System Outline

Nonconformities may occur in manufactured products. All nonconformities are promptly identified, evaluated, segregated (if appropriate), documented, dispositioned and the affected parties notified.

2.12.2 Manufacture

The production manager determines the nature and cause of a nonconformance, determines disposition and advises the functions concerned as appropriate.

Review practices provide for dispositions as follows:

- Rework
- Accept by customer concession
- Regrade for alternate use
- Reject/scrap

Objective evidence is retained to substantiate that any repaired or reworked items have been re-inspected or re-tested as necessary. Records are kept to demonstrate the customer's approval of any concession requests and shall denote the actual condition of the product.

Further specific details are identified in procedure QP.11.

2.13 CORRECTIVE ACTION

2.13.1 System Outline

Corrective action procedures are maintained to:

- investigate causes of nonconforming work or noncompliant system to correct the problem and to prevent a recurrence;
- analyse processes, operations, concessions, records, reports and customer complaints to detect and eliminate potential causes of nonconforming product;
- initiate preventive actions commensurate with the risks involved;
- apply controls to ensure corrective actions are implemented and effective;
- ensure changes to procedures where corrective actions deem it necessary.

2.13.2 Corrective Action Requests

Corrective action requests (CARs) are issued by the quality manager to the relevant production personnel to correct deficiencies in quality.

Corrective action requests may be raised as a result of:

(a) deficiencies found through auditing of the quality system;
(b) "serious" or repetitive "minor" deficiencies in the quality of goods provided;
(c) customer complaints;
(d) management review meetings.

CARs detail the deficiency, the cause(s) of the deficiency, action to be taken to correct the deficiency and the action to be taken to prevent a recurrence of the deficiency.

The quality manager arranges to verify that actions taken to correct the deficiency and prevent recurrence, have been implemented satisfactorily.

Further specific details are identified in procedure QP.12.

2.14 HANDLING, STORAGE, PACKAGING AND DELIVERY

2.14.1 System Outline

Materials and products are handled, stored, packed and delivered in such a manner that prevents damage or deterioration.

2.14.2 Handling

Methods are developed to ensure that items are handled in such a manner as to protect against abuse, misuse, damage, deterioration, contamination or loss.

Where potentially hazardous or sensitive items are received and used, the dangers associated with these items are recognised and appropriate safety precautions taken.

2.14.3 Storage

All chemicals and other purchased goods are stored in identifiable and secure locations. A system for authorising receipt and despatch to and from storage areas is in operation.

Items in storage are inspected periodically to verify condition and shelf life currency (where applicable). Storage conditions and procedures are implemented to prevent damage and deterioration.

2.14.4 Packaging and Packing

Items are protected by preservation and packing to the extent required by the contract or by established procedure to ensure that they conform to specified requirements and do not deteriorate during storage and transit. All packages are identified and marked as required by contract.

2.14.5 Delivery

Items which are delivered to a customer are delivered in such a manner as to prevent loss, damage, or deterioration and ensure timely arrival.

Further specific details are identified in procedure QP.13.

2.15 QUALITY RECORDS

2.15.1 System Outline

Records, including subcontractor records, are identified, collected, indexed, filed, stored, maintained and disposed of in accordance with documented procedures.

Quality records associated with the quality system include, but are not limited to:

(a) system and compliance audit results;
(b) corrective actions;
(c) calibration reports for inspection, measuring and test equipment;
(d) evaluations of suppliers and subcontractors;
(e) training and qualification of personnel;
(f) management review meetings.

2.15.2 Job-related Records

Records associated with the achievement of the desired quality of goods include, but are not limited to:

(a) contract reviews;
(b) inspection and test reports;
(c) nonconformance records;
(d) records relating to purchaser-supplied product;
(e) defect advice notes.

2.15.3 Retention of Records

Accumulated quality records are legible, easily retrieved and stored so as to prevent environmental deterioration or loss.

Records are kept for a minimum period of three years. Where contractually required, records are made available for customer evaluation for the specified period.

Further specific details are identified in procedure QP.14.

2.16 QUALITY AUDITS

2.16.1 System Outline

The quality manager establishes an audit programme within the company which objectively evaluates the adequacy and effectiveness of the functions and procedures referenced in this manual. The frequency of audits is planned on the basis of the status and importance of the activity to be verified.

Audits include an evaluation of:

(a) quality practices and procedures;
(b) documentation and records;
(c) work areas, processes, operator capabilities and goods produced;
(d) suppliers.

Audits are performed in accordance with documented audit procedures using appropriate audit checklists.

Audits are carried out by trained personnel who are not directly responsible for the area being audited.

Personnel responsible for the area being audited review, agree and correct deficiencies revealed in the audit in a timely manner.

All audits are documented.

Actions taken to correct deficiencies are followed up to verify compliance.

Further specific details are identified in procedure QP.15.

2.17 TRAINING

2.17.1 System Outline

Procedures for identifying the training requirements for all staff performing activities affecting quality are identified, categorised and documented.

2.17.2 General Training

All personnel have their work skills assessed and recorded during the initial job interviews. Personnel files to hold this information are opened and maintained for all company employees.

The company implements suitable training programmes to ensure all employees receive instructions in the company's policies and practices.

The company maintains suitable training programmes to ensure all employees receive instructions appropriate to their level of skill and to the work tasks they are to perform.

Training needs are analysed on an ongoing basis during management review.

2.17.3 Training in quality assurance

All company personnel receive instruction in the policy and objectives of the company's quality system.

Appropriate training records are maintained.

Further specific details are identified in procedure QP.16.

2.18 SERVICING

2.18.1 System Outline

Where servicing is a contractual requirement, procedures are developed and maintained to ensure that service work is performed, reported and verified against specified requirements.

2.18.2 Servicing Control

Where work has been completed and the contract includes servicing, a product service manual is produced to ensure that the product continues to operate between services.

The service manual will be developed on a time/distance schedule and will be maintained with the product as a historical record of work and to confirm verification of servicing.

2.19 STATISTICAL TECHNIQUES

2.19.1 System Outline

Process control capabilities and product characteristics are monitored as appropriate using basic statistical methods.

2.19.2 Statistical Process Monitoring

Nonconformities are monitored statistically to reveal trends in process performance. Nonconformance records are plotted collectively as a ratio of:

(a) products produced per month;
(b) manhours required for rework, repair and downtime associated with nonconformances.

Further specific details are identified in procedure QP.17.

3.0 PROCEDURES INDEX

ABC Co. has documented procedures for all systems and functions that apply to the quality programme.

Each procedure identifies, as applicable, such things as its purpose and scope, "who" is responsible for "what", "how", "when", and "where".

The ABC Co.'s list of quality system procedures are as follows:

Procedure title	Procedure no.
Writing a Quality System and Work Procedure	QP.01
Management Review	QP.02
Contract Review	QP.03
Document Control	QP.04
Purchasing	QP.05
Purchaser-supplied Product	QP.06
Product Identification and Traceability	QP.07
Process Control	QP.08
Receiving Inspection and Testing	QP.09A
In-process and Final Inspection and Testing	QP.09B
Inspection, Measuring and Test Equipment	QP.10
Control of Nonconforming Product	QP.11
Corrective Action	QP.12
Handling, Storage, Packaging and Delivery	QP.13
Quality Records	QP.14
Internal Quality Audits	QP.15
Training	QP.16
Statistical Process Monitoring	QP.17

STEP 3

PLANNING

3.1 PRELIMINARY REVIEW

Before embarking on a full-scale "clean slate" approach, the first activity you should undertake is an examination of your company's current processes and systems in order to conduct an evaluation against the requirements of the appropriate standard. You may be pleasantly surprised at the extent to which you have already got some sort of a quality system in place, although the likelihood is that it is not documented, or you may get a shock! In any event, the purpose of the preliminary review is to enable you to make an assessment of the time scale and resources required to put the quality system in place.

The easiest and most practical way of carrying out the preliminary review is to start at the bottom and follow these suggested steps:

(a) Identify and collect together all the existing forms, charts (e.g. organisation charts, flowcharts, schedules), work instructions, any procedures (in whatever format), etc., for all departments or functions within the company. You can either use blank forms or, preferably, copies of actual forms used, as examples.

(b) Using the list of quality system "elements" in the relevant standard and the descriptions outlined in Step 2, sort all the above documents into a system element category – there are twenty applicable elements in ISO 9001, eighteen in ISO 9002 and twelve in ISO 9003. You may find that some documents relate to more than one element, in which case you should make additional copies or cross-refer by way of a note.

(c) Prepare a checklist report, along the lines of the example in Table 2, to identify deficiencies and duplications in the present system. Procedures which are stated as being specifically required in the standard (ISO 9002) are classified here as "mandatory", and procedures which we believe are required in addition to these are classified as "essential". The combined list is what we believe to be *minimum* requirements for most companies and you may well have additional procedures. For each procedure on the list, briefly reference any existing forms, work instructions, procedures, etc., which relate in whole or in part to it. If your existing forms or procedures do not have reference numbers, give them some sort of temporary reference for now. Make notes, either in the "comments" section or on separate sheets to describe the extent to which you think the form or procedure meets any of the requirements of the standard.

(d) From the above checklist and analysis, prepare a report in as much detail as possible, identifying deficiencies, weaknesses, gaps, etc., by quality system element and, if possible by department or function. Bear in mind that gaps against mandatory procedures are major omissions and gaps against essential procedures may be major or minor depending on the extent of the omission (i.e. major or minor in the context of certification).

Table 2 Preliminary review: procedure checklist

ISO 9002 CLAUSE	PROCEDURE REQUIRED	M or E*	EXISTING DOCUMENTATION		
			FORMS/CHARTS	WORK PROCEDURES	SYSTEM PROCEDURES
4.1	Management Review	E			
4.2	Preparation of System Procedures	E			
4.3	Contract Review	M			
4.4	Control of Quality Manuals, Procedures, Work Instructions and Forms	M			
4.4	Control of National Standards, Specifications and Technical Documents	M			
4.4	Control of Correspondence	M			
4.6	Supplier/Subcontractor Assessment	E			
4.6	Purchase Orders	E			
4.7	Purchaser-supplied Product (where relevant)	M			
4.8	Product Identification and Traceability (where appropriate)	M			
4.9	Production and Installation Planning	E			
4.9	Preparation of Work Procedures	E			
4.9	Special Processes (where relevant)	M			
4.10	Receiving Inspection and Testing	M			
4.10	In-process Inspection and Testing	M			
4.10	Final Inspection and Testing	M			
4.11	Calibration and Control of Inspection, Measuring and Test Equipment	M			
4.13	Control of Nonconforming Product	M			
4.14	Corrective Action	M			
4.15	Handling, Storage, Packaging and Delivery	M			
4.16	Control of Quality Records	M			
4.17	Internal Quality Audits	M			
4.18	Training Needs and Provision	M			
4.19	Servicing	M			
4.20	Statistical Techniques (where appropriate)	M			

*M = Mandatory   E = Essential

You must also realise that you are probably carrying out this preliminary review with little or no experience of quality system requirements and, to a large extent, you may have to make judgements about how satisfactory or otherwise your current forms and procedures are. Nevertheless, it is a vital part of the quality system process as well as being a good source of learning experience.

3.2 QUALITY SYSTEM DEVELOPMENT SCHEDULE

The findings of the preliminary review will provide the basis for a schedule plan to be developed which will indicate the requirements for personnel and resources and the likely schedule for implementation of the quality system.

The importance of this planning phase cannot be stressed enough; too many companies set "target" dates for certification and then work backwards causing unbelievable levels of friction which only works against their quality objectives.

The development schedule should take into account the amount of time the quality representative and other members of the steering committee can reasonably devote to the quality programme. This, in turn may be a function of your company's cash flow situation. You should consider the final certification timetable in the light of the fluctuation or seasonality of your operations and even the likely holidays of key personnel. Don't forget that the assessors will make surveillance visits twice a year, so you cannot always plan them to coincide with the "good" times.

From the preliminary report, you should be able to make a reasonable estimate of how many procedures you need to prepare and how long each one will take to write, check, review, approve, implement and audit. Again, bear in mind that the review process can be lengthy if the procedure involves interfaces between various personnel.

An example of a quality system development schedule is shown in Figure 7. The time scales are indications only.

The development schedule should be produced as a formal document, subject to revision status and an approval mechanism. It should be approved by the managing director and alterations/revisions to the plan should also be subject to the same approval. The schedule will form the working document of the steering committee.

3.3 CERTIFICATION

Step 7 deals with the certification process in detail. It is mentioned here to act as a reminder for early contact to be made with the assessors to discuss their time scales and schedules. Once you have an action plan in place you may wish to consider discussing it with the assessors and making a provisional "booking" if necessary.

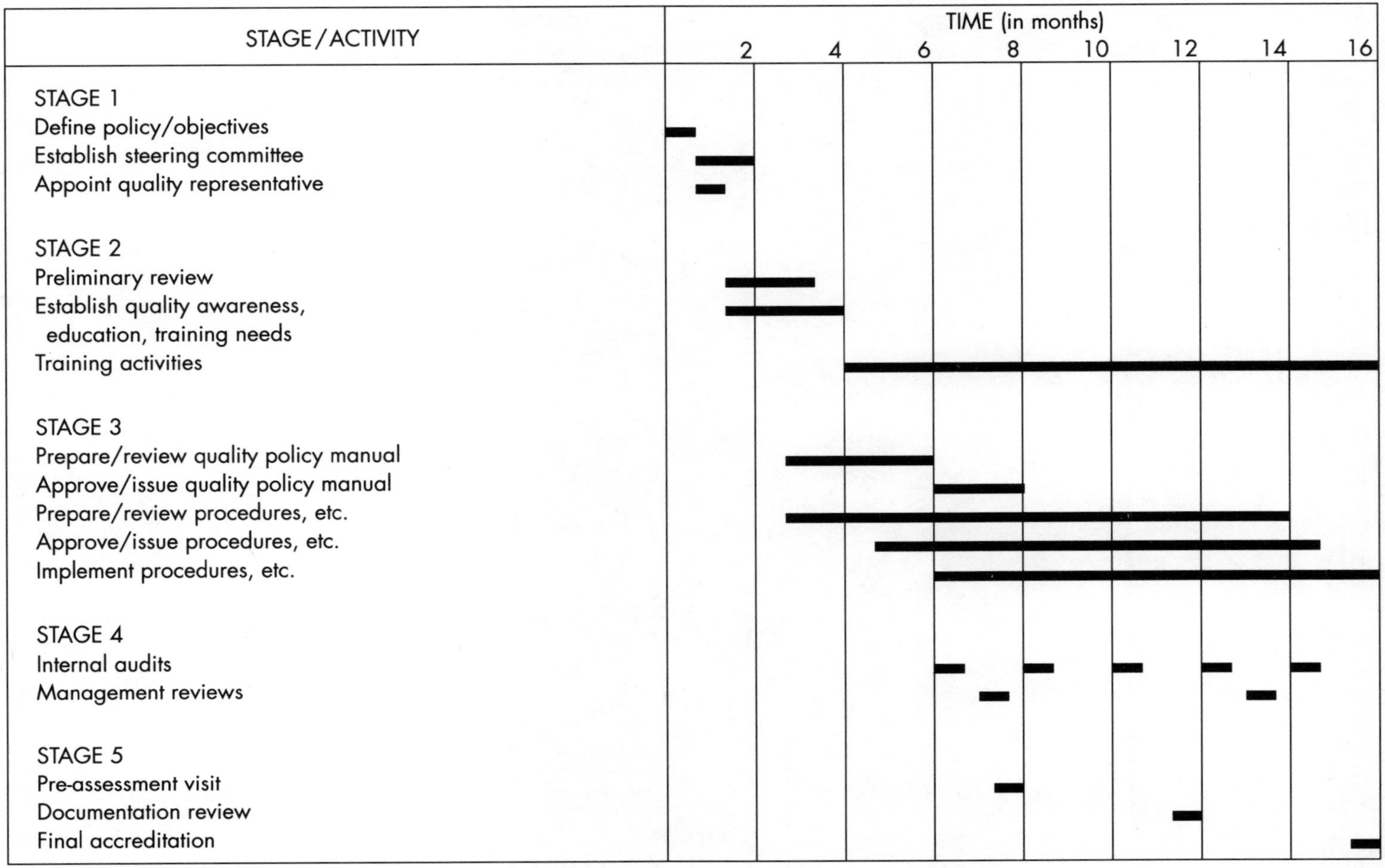
STAGE / ACTIVITY
TIME (in months)
2
4
6
8
10
12
14
16
STAGE 1
Define policy/objectives
Establish steering committee
Appoint quality representative
STAGE 2
Preliminary review
Establish quality awareness, education, training needs
Training activities
STAGE 3
Prepare/review quality policy manual
Approve/issue quality policy manual
Prepare/review procedures, etc.
Approve/issue procedures, etc.
Implement procedures, etc.
STAGE 4
Internal audits
Management reviews
STAGE 5
Pre-assessment visit
Documentation review
Final accreditation

Figure 7 Quality system development schedule

STEP 4

TRAINING, EDUCATION AND QUALITY AWARENESS

4.1 ORGANISATION AND RESPONSIBILITIES

To be effective, the quality system has to work within the framework of an organisation that clearly defines reporting relationships and how responsibility and authority are delegated. Very often, this is an area which is overlooked or ignored when considering a quality system. Too much emphasis may be given to the quality of the *output* of the system and not enough to the quality of the *input*, i.e. people.

All employees need to know:

- where they fit into the overall organisation;
- what their functional or departmental lines of reporting and communication are;
- what their detailed responsibilities and limits of authority are.

Similarly, managers need to be able to:

- delegate responsibilities to suitably qualified and experienced personnel;
- communicate job requirements in a clear, consistent fashion;
- assess performance in accordance with objective, agreed criteria.

The most effective way of meeting these needs is to document and issue organisation charts and job descriptions (and, of course, procedures which are covered in Step 5).

Organisation charts and job descriptions should be prepared and issued as formal documents in the same way as procedures and other quality system documentation. They should be dated, numbered/referenced, given revision status indicators and approved (signed) by appropriate managers.

Organisation charts should be prepared in a sequential manner, starting with the Board of Directors or senior level of management and working down to the shop-floor level. Prepare as many charts as necessary and split on a departmental or activity basis as appropriate. Generally, each chart should be approved by the person whose name heads the top level on the chart. A sample organisation chart format is shown in Figure 8. Each employee should be issued with a copy of the chart on which his/her position appears and should be made aware of the existence of a full set of company organisation charts.

Job descriptions should also be prepared in a consistent fashion for every position on the organisation charts. (*Note:* Some employees may perform more than one function, e.g. one person as purchasing manager and quality manager.) Each job description should include details of:

- position title;
- reporting to (immediate superior);
- qualifications, skills and experience required;
- primary job function;

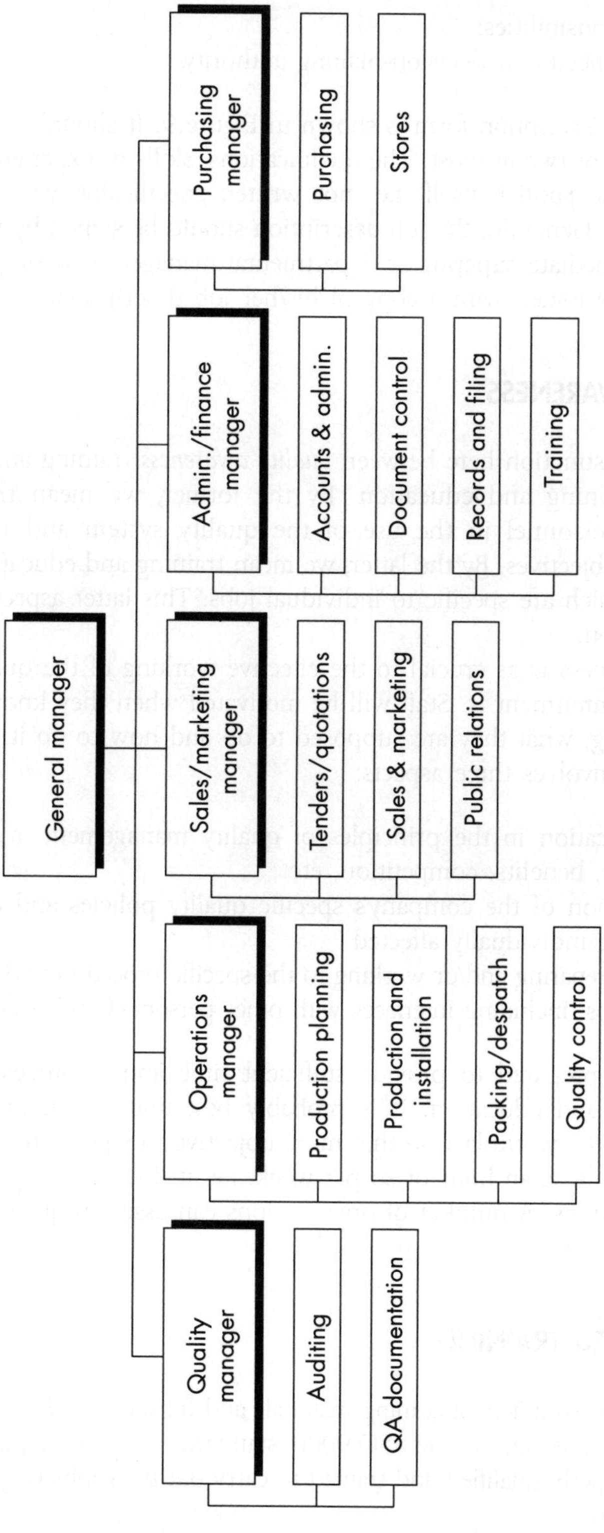
General manager
Quality manager
Auditing
QA documentation
Operations manager
Production planning
Production and installation
Packing/despatch
Quality control
Sales/marketing manager
Tenders/quotations
Sales & marketing
Public relations
Admin./finance manager
Accounts & admin.
Document control
Records and filing
Training
Purchasing manager
Purchasing
Stores

Figure 8 Company organisation chart

- detailed responsibilities;
- limits of financial and decision-making authority.

A sample job description form is shown in Figure 9. It should generally only comprise one page, or two at most. The qualifications, skills or experience required should relate to the *position* itself, i.e. not written specifically with the present incumbent in mind. Generally, the job description should be signed by the position holder and the immediate superior or departmental manager, as appropriate. Each employee should be issued with a copy of his/her job description(s).

4.2 QUALITY AWARENESS

We have made a distinction here between *quality awareness* training and education and *job-specific* training and education. By the former, we mean training and education of all personnel in the use of the quality system and meeting the company's quality objectives. By the latter, we mean training and education in skills or qualifications which are specific to individual jobs. This latter aspect is covered in 4.3 of this section.

Quality awareness is as crucial to the effective working of the quality system as management commitment is. Staff will be motivated when they know why they are doing something, what they are supposed to do and how to do it. Training in quality awareness involves three aspects:

- General education in the principles of quality management, e.g. customer requirements, benefits, competition, etc.
- Communication of the company's specific quality policies and objectives – how they are individually affected
- Training in preparing and/or working to the specific procedures which relate to individual jobs, including interfaces with other personnel and responsibilities

You must be prepared to provide sufficient time and resources for quality awareness training and education. It is probably best undertaken in sessions or courses away from the workplace so that more objective thought can be provoked. This could be as little as an hour or so per week, i.e. it does not mean a full-scale shutdown of operations. A number of organisations can assist in quality awareness development – see 4.4.

4.3 JOB-ORIENTED TRAINING

In the same way that suppliers, incoming materials and finished products are assessed against measurable criteria, so the ISO 9000 standards include requirements for personnel to be properly qualified and trained to carry out their jobs (e.g. clause 4.18

JOB DESCRIPTION	No.: ________ Rev.: ________
Title: ____________________	
Primary function: ____________________ ____________________ Scope of duties: ____________________ ____________________ ____________________ ____________________ ____________________ ____________________	
Responsible to: ____________________	
Subordinate staff directly supervised: ____________________ ____________________ ____________________	Subordinate staff indirectly supervised: ____________________ ____________________ ____________________
Limits of authority: ____________________ ____________________ ____________________	
Qualifications required: ____________________ ____________________ ____________________ ____________________ Experience required: ____________________ ____________________ ____________________ Skills required: ____________________ ____________________ ____________________ ____________________ Personal qualities required: ____________________ ____________________ ____________________	
Prepared by: Approved by:	Date: Date:

Figure 9 Sample job description form

Q.A. Management Services Pty. Ltd.	EMPLOYEE TRAINING RECORD		
Name:		Position:	
Principal duties:			
Education and qualifications:		Membership of professional bodies/institutions:	
TRAINING – INTERNAL AND EXTERNAL			
DATE/ DURATION	COURSE TITLE	DESCRIPTION OF TRAINING	TRAINING PROVIDER

Figure 10 An employee training record

of ISO 9002). Evidence is required that the specified criteria are met, which means maintaining training records, details of qualifications and job descriptions (see 4.1 earlier). Such records can be audited. An example of an employee training record for course attendance is shown in Figure 10.

Job-oriented training should be carried out in a structured fashion and should relate to the needs of the job. If the training is "on-the-job" and, for example, an operator is training under a supervisor, the activities being carried out and the criteria for acceptance should be laid down and signed off by the supervisor once the course or training period is complete.

4.4 TRAINING COURSES

There are a number of organisations in the marketplace offering quality-related courses. Many of these courses are designed to provide the quality practitioner with the theoretical means of developing and implementing a quality system, e.g. how to prepare a quality manual and associated procedures. Some of the organisations are able to offer specially-tailored in-house courses which may be more appropriate for your company if you are already implementing a quality system by means of this handbook. Relevant in-house courses might be on aspects such as customer needs, quality cost-benefit analysis, auditor training, etc.

STEP 5

QUALITY SYSTEM AND WORK PROCEDURES

5.1 PURPOSE OF PROCEDURES

Referring again to the hierarchy of quality system documentation, the second and third levels of documentation are the more detailed quality system procedures and work procedures, respectively, which flow down from the quality policy manual. The hierarchy diagram is shown in Figure 11 for ease of reference.

Just as the quality policy manual defines *what* the company's quality policies and objectives are, so the procedures detail *who* does *what* and *why*, *where*, *when* and *how* it is done. Work procedures are even more specific in terms of detailing *how* certain process activities are to be performed and *what with*. Forms and records provide the documentary inputs and outputs of the quality system.

The distinction between a system procedure and a work procedure is generally made on the basis of the interfaces and responsibilities involved. A system procedure will usually involve interfaces between two or more persons, or departments and will detail various responsibilities and authorities for the sequenced activities. A work procedure will usually detail the step-by-step approach to carrying out a specific activity and may only apply to one person or department in the company. By way of an example, in an engineering-type company there may be a *system procedure* for the review and approval of drawings which will detail who prepares them, who checks and approves them, where they are maintained and who updates the register, etc.; there may then be a *work procedure* detailing how the drawing itself should be prepared, including reference numbers, the symbols to be used, how to identify changes, etc.

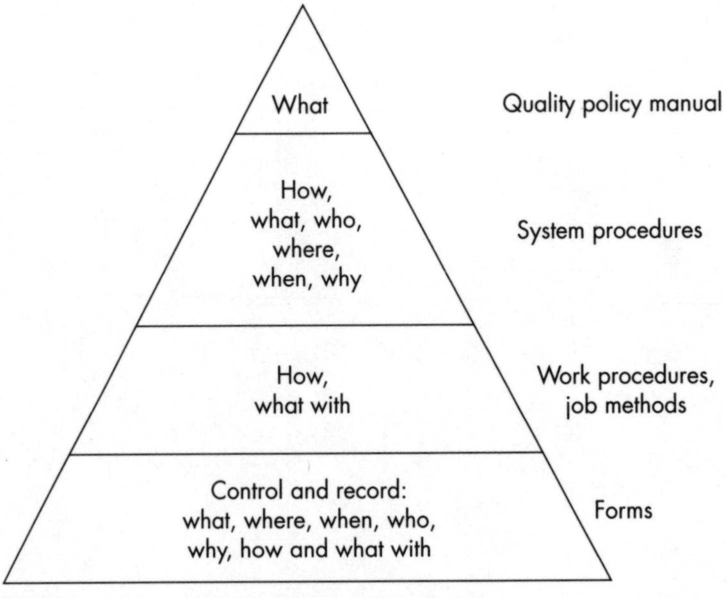
What
Quality policy manual
How,
what, who,
where,
when, why
System procedures
How,
what with
Work procedures,
job methods
Control and record:
what, where, when, who,
why, how and what with
Forms

Figure 11 Quality system documentation

The need to document processes and activities in the form of system procedures and work procedures is:

- to ensure uniformity in performing tasks and activities;
- to enable audit and assessment of the quality system against measurable standards;
- to clearly define responsibilities and authority levels;
- to control changes in operating methods and practices.

5.2 SCOPE OF PROCEDURES

The above list of reasons for having procedures is not exhaustive, but neither does it imply that every single activity carried out in the company must be fully documented. The control of documentation is in itself a very important part of the quality system and it must therefore be manageable.

The decision as to which processes and activities you should document must be arrived at by working down through the quality policy manual's objectives rather than working up from the individual processes. Therefore, use the concept of the quality system documentation hierarchy to define, structure and cross-refer all levels of documentation.

If you refer back to Step 3, you will find a checklist of procedures which we believe to be minimum requirements for most companies. We have classified as "mandatory" those which are stated as being specifically required in the standard (ISO 9002) and additional procedures are classified as being "essential".

Model system procedures corresponding to this list are included at the end of Step 5. These system procedures have been written in a very general sense and the purpose of including them in this handbook is as a starting point and a framework for you to develop your own company-specific procedures. Nevertheless, some procedures can be virtually adapted "as is", i.e. they are almost universal in their application – e.g. preparation of procedures, internal auditing, etc.

A list of basic system procedures is included at the back of the model quality policy manual to cross-reference the documentation.

5.3 PREPARATION AND FORMAT OF SYSTEM PROCEDURES

Having established the need for a particular system procedure and the scope and objectives of the procedure, the development thereafter involves the following five steps:

- Identifying current practice
- Documenting current practice

- Reviewing current practice and revising as necessary
- Preparing the procedure
- Authorising and issuing the procedure

It is important to stress that your system procedures and work procedures should reflect current practices within your company (provided they conform with the standard, of course) and not what you would ideally like to be doing! Remember that they will be audited. Neither should you fall into the trap of writing procedures for activities which you do not perform.

5.3.1 Identify Current Practice

In order to complete this aspect of system developments, the following stages should be followed:

- Identify current methods of performing the activities and identify responsibilities and the documentation and equipment in use.
- Determine current standards of acceptability, if any, which are applied and assess how effectively they are being achieved.
- Identify critical aspects of the activities, particularly those affecting quality.

5.3.2 Document Current Practice

Having identified current practices you should document them in a clear and precise format to facilitate subsequent review.

In order to structure the documented, current practice into correct sequences it is important to know how each activity is carried out, how each step is initiated and how it leads into the next.

Simple flowcharts such as the example shown in Figure 12 may be of assistance provided their use is consistent. Flowcharting can be especially effective in those cases where personnel undertaking a description of their current activities may not normally be called upon to perform writing duties or where use of the local language may be a problem.

5.3.3 Review Current Practice

Review of the documented current practices together with any proposals for change should be done by the steering committee (see Step 1) together with the appropriate responsible personnel in order to assess and determine whether:

- specified objectives are being achieved;

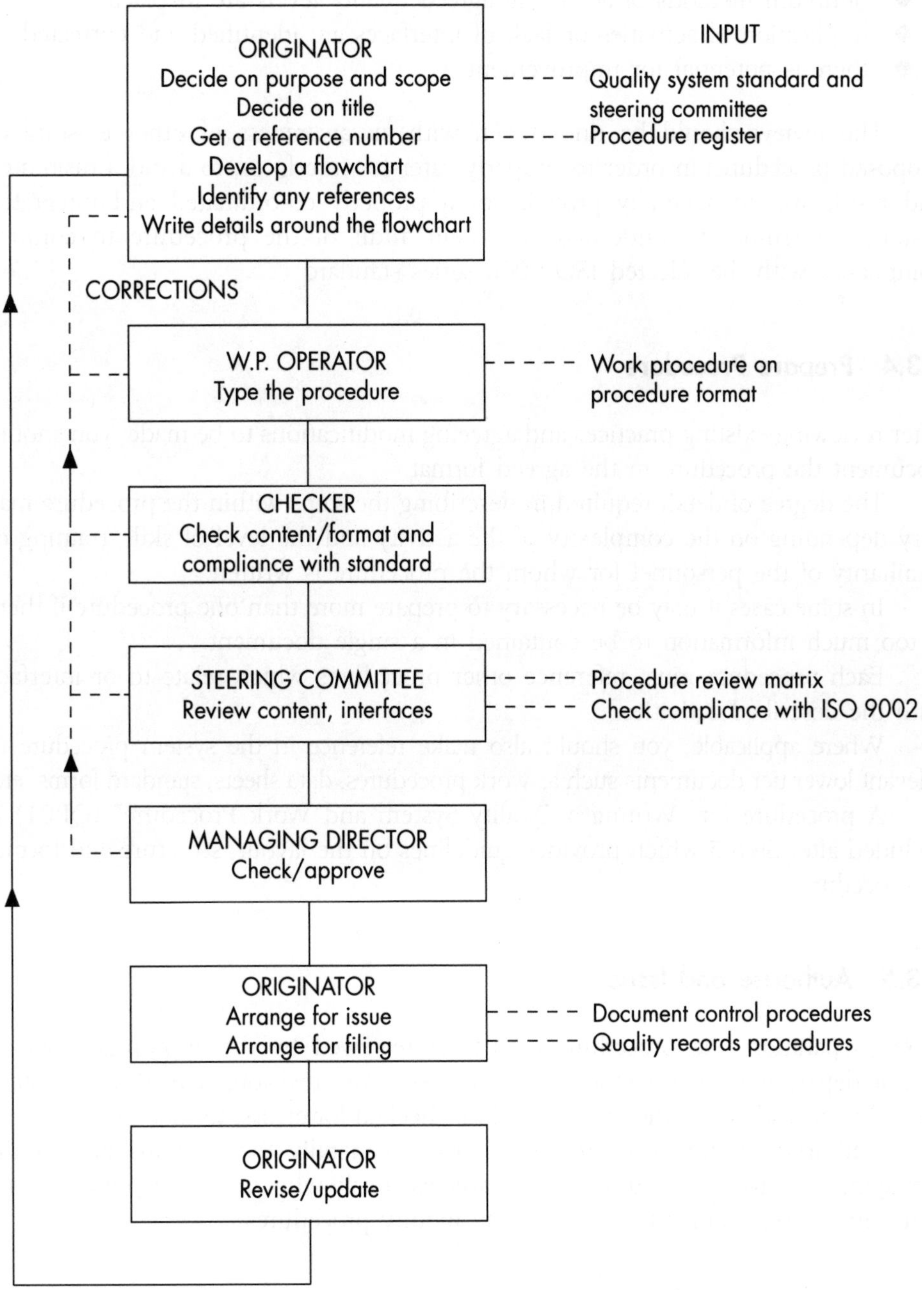
ORIGINATOR
Decide on purpose and scope
Decide on title
Get a reference number
Develop a flowchart
Identify any references
Write details around the flowchart
INPUT
Quality system standard and steering committee
Procedure register
CORRECTIONS
W.P. OPERATOR
Type the procedure
Work procedure on procedure format
CHECKER
Check content/format and compliance with standard
STEERING COMMITTEE
Review content, interfaces
Procedure review matrix
Check compliance with ISO 9002
MANAGING DIRECTOR
Check/approve
ORIGINATOR
Arrange for issue
Arrange for filing
Document control procedures
Quality records procedures
ORIGINATOR
Revise/update

Figure 12 Flowchart for the preparation of procedures

- appropriate methods are in use;
- quality levels are adequate;
- optimum methods of achieving agreed quality levels are in place;
- duplication of activities or lack of interfaces are identified and corrected;
- there is potential for improvement.

The review should be undertaken with an awareness of other existing or proposed procedures in order to properly cater for interfaces, to avoid a disjointed end result and to generally provide for a properly co-ordinated and integrated system. Remember to undertake a system audit of the procedure to confirm compliance with the selected ISO 9000 series standard.

5.3.4 Prepare Procedure

After reviewing existing practices and agreeing modifications to be made, you should document the procedure in the agreed format.

The degree of detail required in describing the steps within the procedure may vary depending on the complexity of the activity and the level of skill, training or familiarity of the personnel for whom the procedure is written.

In some cases it may be necessary to prepare more than one procedure if there is too much information to be contained in a single document.

Each procedure must reference other procedures which relate to or interface with the described activities.

Where applicable, you should also make reference in the system procedure to relevant lower tier documents such as work procedures, data sheets, standard forms, etc.

A procedure for "Writing a Quality System and Work Procedure" (QP.01) is included after Step 5 which provides guidelines on the layout, structure and format of procedures.

5.3.5 Authorise and Issue

After preparation, the procedure should be reviewed by the appropriate person and/or department for operational effectiveness. Any revisions agreed at this stage should be recorded and the final procedure checked for errors, format and structure.

Authorisation for issue of procedures is generally the responsibility of the managing director but you should clearly establish who in the organisation has authority to issue, amend or in any way modify procedures.

5.4 PREPARATION OF WORK PROCEDURES

It is difficult to give detailed guidelines on the preparation, format, style, etc., of work procedures as they can take many forms and can be prepared for many different types of activities. For example, a work procedure can be in the form of a memo, a specification, a job method sheet, an operating manual, or several other forms. Work procedures can range from activities such as filling in time sheets to operating a complex piece of machinery.

The main guidelines which should be taken into account in the preparation and use of work procedures are derived from the requirements of the standard for documentation control (sections 4.4, 4.9 and 4.18 of ISO 9002). These requirements are summarised simply as:

- having the correct issues of documents available to those personnel who need to use the information or data to perform their duties;
- having specific work procedures, where the absence of such procedures would adversely affect quality;
- providing appropriate training for specific jobs and tasks.

For work procedures, therefore, this means that you should adopt standard methods for referencing, dating, approving and issuing. Given the potential number and variety of work procedures you must give careful thought to which ones are deemed to be included in the quality system documentation. That will depend on the nature and complexity of your business, the amount of formal training which personnel have undergone and the implications of not having written work procedures on the quality of the final product.

The standard also requires a master list or equivalent documentation control mechanism to be established, so that the correct revisions of documents can be readily identified by all. This should include work procedures.

5.5 RESPONSIBILITIES

Allocating responsibility for developing and writing the procedures themselves is almost always a difficult decision – a balance between choosing people who are familiar and comfortable with writing and documenting activities and people who are likely to be performing the activities and actually working to these procedures. Try to involve the latter category as much as possible in identifying current practices, methods, interfaces and in checking and testing procedures.

ABC COMPANY

QUALITY SYSTEM PROCEDURE

FOR

WRITING QUALITY SYSTEM AND WORK PROCEDURES

DOCUMENT NO.: QP.01

	NAME	SIGNATURE	DATE
PREPARED BY:			
APPROVED BY:			

Copy no.: ______________

Controlled ( )

Uncontrolled ( )

TABLE OF CONTENTS

ISSUE HISTORY

ISSUE NO.	DATE	DESCRIPTION	REVISED BY	APPROVED BY
A	23 August 1993	Issued		

1.0 PURPOSE

This procedure defines the standard requirements for the preparation and format of quality system and work procedures used by the ABC Company.

2.0 SCOPE

This procedure applies to all system and work procedures developed by the ABC Company to identify the activities and responsibilities of employees in tasks affecting quality.

3.0 DEFINITIONS

3.1 Quality System Procedure

A clear and specific documented description of an activity including (as applicable) personnel responsibilities, the sequence of events, methods to be employed, equipment to be used, and when and where the foregoing applies.

3.2 Work Procedures

A simple document or flow chart providing step-by-step instructions on how to perform a specific task. Personnel responsibilities are not necessarily defined, as work procedures may be used by any employee within the company.

3.3 Senior Personnel

Line management reporting directly to the managing director.

4.0 REFERENCE MATERIAL

QP.04 – Document Control

5.0 RESPONSIBILITIES

5.1 Quality Manager

The quality manager shall be responsible for the generation and control of all quality system documentation. The quality manager may delegate these tasks to suitably qualified personnel.

5.2 Senior Personnel

Senior personnel shall report any quality-related issues to the quality manager for advice and guidance on their resolution. This may involve identifying the need for a new or revised quality system and work procedures.

5.3 Managing Director

The managing director has the sole responsibility and authority for approving quality system procedures. Work procedures may be approved by any senior personnel.

6.0 PROCEDURE

6.1 Quality System Documents

The need to write a quality system procedure shall generally be determined by the quality manager. The need for a work procedure shall generally be determined by senior personnel and will generally be used in their area of responsibility to clarify or describe how to perform a straightforward task usually involving one person or one item of equipment. However, senior personnel and/or the management review committee may recognise the need for additional procedures and should bring this to the attention of the quality manager for consideration.

6.2 Quality System Procedure Numbering

The quality system procedure shall be provided with a unique identification number as listed in the quality policy manual. Unlisted or new procedures shall be assigned a number obtained from the quality manager.

6.3 Procedure Content

6.3.1 Title Page

All procedures shall have a title page (page 1) which shall contain the following information:

- Company name
- Procedure title
- Procedure number
- Name, signature and date of the persons who prepare and approve the procedure
- Copy number
- Indication of whether the procedure is controlled or uncontrolled

6.3.2 Contents Page

The contents page (page 2) shall contain the following information:

- Table of contents
- Issue history indicating issue number, date, description of revision and initials of the persons who revised and approved the amendment

6.3.3 Headers

All pages from page 2 onwards shall contain headers with the following information: the company's name "ABC Company", the page number out of total pages, document number, date of issue, issue identifier and procedure title.

6.3.4 General Contents

All quality system procedure contents shall be written under the following sections and headings:

1.0 PURPOSE
Outlining the objectives or intention of the quality system procedure.

2.0 SCOPE

Defining the sphere, department or personnel to which the quality system procedure applies and the limits of its application.

3.0 DEFINITIONS

Explaining words, phrases terminology or actions which may not be universally understood. This section is optional and may point to an industry standard such as ISO 8402.

4.0 REFERENCE MATERIAL

Listing other documents which also apply to the activities described within the quality system procedure and are specifically referred to for further details.

5.0 RESPONSIBILITIES

Identifying by position or title those persons having functions to perform within the quality system procedure and their respective duties.

6.0 PROCEDURE

Detailing sequential requirements and the necessary actions of personnel involved in the activities defined. This section identifies who does what, when, where and how.

APPENDIXES

Any pertinent documents, pro-formas, etc., which are required in order to perform the functions detailed in the quality system procedure.

6.4 Issuance of Quality System Procedure

New quality system procedures shall be reviewed by the quality manager and approved by the managing director, prior to being issued in accordance with procedure QP.04.

6.5 Revision of Quality System Procedures

Where change to quality system procedures becomes necessary, the quality system procedures shall be revised and completely re-issued in accordance with procedure QP.04.

Revisions and replacement of individual pages shall not apply for quality system procedures.

6.6 Work Procedures

6.6.1 Specific tasks such as operating a machine or following certain conventions may not require the level of detail and formality demanded by a quality system procedure. Work procedures may therefore be prepared as simple flowcharts or step-by-step documents that "walk" the reader through the performance of a task (e.g. how to strip a machine for servicing or how to complete a form).

In these cases a work procedure proforma sheet (QP.01.01) shall be completed defining the following:

- Work procedure number and issue status from the register of work procedures maintained by document control (QP.04)
- Title
- Equipment/material – this section defines all the necessary equipment, materials or skills necessary prior to commencing the work
- Operations – outlining the step number and a description of the operation
- Controlled/uncontrolled status – defining whether the copy is controlled as defined in QP.04
- Prepared by – signature of the document author
- Approved by – signature of the managing director or senior personnel

Work procedures shall always include the acceptance criteria for workmanship where applicable, which will provide the user with defined limits of acceptability by value or representative sample.

Work procedures are registered and issued on a controlled basis as defined in QP.04.

APPENDIX

Work Procedure Proforma (QP.01.01)

APPENDIX

WORK PROCEDURE	No.: Page:	Issue: of

Title:

Equipment/Materials:

OPERATIONS	
NO.	DESCRIPTION

Controlled (   )

Copy no. _____ Prepared by: ___________ Date: ___________

Uncontrolled (   ) Approved by: ___________ Date: ___________

QP.01.01 Version 1

ABC COMPANY

QUALITY SYSTEM PROCEDURE

FOR

MANAGEMENT REVIEW

DOCUMENT NO.: QP.02

	NAME	SIGNATURE	DATE
PREPARED BY:			
APPROVED BY:			

Copy no.: ______________

Controlled ( )

Uncontrolled ( )

TABLE OF CONTENTS

ISSUE HISTORY

ISSUE NO.	DATE	DESCRIPTION	REVISED BY	APPROVED BY
A	10 August 1993	Issued		

1.0 PURPOSE

The purpose of this quality system procedure is to provide the method of periodic review of the quality system by management to ensure its continuing suitability and effectiveness.

2.0 SCOPE

This quality system procedure applies to reviews of the quality management system performed by senior management.

3.0 DEFINITIONS

Nil

4.0 REFERENCE MATERIAL

QP.04 – Document Control
QP.12 – Corrective Action
QP.15 – Internal Quality Audits

5.0 RESPONSIBILITIES

5.1 Quality Manager

The quality manager is responsible for the following:

(a) Convening management review meetings
(b) Preparing an agenda for the meetings
(c) Maintaining records of management review meetings
(d) Initiating resolutions resulting from meetings

5.2 Senior Management

Senior management are responsible for attending meetings upon request from the quality manager. This will include, as a minimum, the following personnel:

(a) Managing director
(b) Production manager
(c) Quality manager
(d) Purchasing officer

6.0 PROCEDURE

6.1 Initiation of Review

The quality manager shall identify the need for a management review meeting, based on any of the following criteria:

(a) Six-monthly interval elapsed
(b) Excessive customer complaints
(c) Serious quality issues or statistical trends requiring a review of the quality system

6.2 Initiation of Review Meetings

Upon identifying this need, the quality manager shall convene the meeting by summoning all relevant senior personnel as detailed in 5.2.

6.3 Review Agenda

The meeting shall be used to review and evaluate the entire quality system to re-affirm its adequacy and conformance to current requirements of the company.

Each review meeting will address the following matters; the personnel responsible for collecting data for the meeting are identified also:

(a) Internal quality audit reports	Quality manager
(b) External audit reports	Quality manager
(c) Customer complaints	Managing director
(d) Employee feedback	Production manager
(e) Outstanding corrective action	Quality manager
(f) Training needs	All attendees
(g) Supplier performance	Purchasing officer
(h) Statistical trends	Quality manager
(i) Minutes of the previous meeting and the outcome of all assigned actions	Quality manager

6.4 Documentation of Review

The quality manager shall record minutes of all discussion items and resolutions. The quality manager shall issue copies of the minutes to other personnel as appropriate, where action is required.

Minutes of review meetings shall be retained by the quality manager.

6.5 Implementation of Resolutions

Some resolutions may result in a change to work practices and/or procedures. In such cases all relevant manuals and procedures will be revised and reissued as defined in QP.04.

Where management identifies a problem during the meeting, it shall be the responsibility of the quality manager to initiate corrective action in accordance with QP.12.

When management identifies a problem, but cannot determine the precise root cause, then the quality manager shall arrange an unscheduled internal quality audit in accordance with QP.15 to pinpoint the problem.

ABC COMPANY

QUALITY SYSTEM PROCEDURE

FOR

CONTRACT REVIEW

DOCUMENT NO.: QP.03

	NAME	SIGNATURE	DATE
PREPARED BY:			
APPROVED BY:			

Copy no.: ____________

Controlled ( )

Uncontrolled ( )

TABLE OF CONTENTS

ISSUE HISTORY

ISSUE NO.	DATE	DESCRIPTION	REVISED BY	APPROVED BY
A	10 August 1993	Issued		

1.0 PURPOSE

The purposes of this procedure are:

- to ensure that the requirements of all contracts are adequately understood, defined, and documented;
- to ensure that ABC Company has the capability to meet contractual requirements;
- to establish and initiate the planning of work after acceptance of the contract;
- to ensure that all differences between the tender and contract are resolved with the customer.

2.0 SCOPE

This quality system procedure applies to activities involved in the submission of quotations and/or tender bids for contracts through to acceptance of the order.

3.0 DEFINITIONS

3.1 Tender

Any enquiry or request for quotation.

3.2 Contract

All orders placed on the company.

3.3 Sales and Marketing Manager

Any person within the company responsible for preparing quotations and processing incoming orders.

4.0 REFERENCE MATERIAL

QP.09B – In-process and Final Inspection and Testing
QP.15 – Internal Quality Audits

5.0 RESPONSIBILITIES

5.1 Managing Director

The managing director is responsible for:

(a) nominating the sales and marketing manager;
(b) reviewing and approving tenders.

5.2 Sales and Marketing Manager

The sales and marketing manager is responsible for:

(a) reviewing customer enquiries, preparing quotations, and processing customer change orders;
(b) liaising with other departments or suppliers to ensure the timely completion of all work under the order;
(c) administration of the order;
(d) maintaining the job number register;
(e) identifying and listing, into the job file, purchaser-supplied product.

5.3 Quality Manager

The quality manager is responsible for:

(a) providing quality related information for inclusion in tender bids;
(b) assisting in the preparation or review of a quality plan for the order.

6.0 PROCEDURE

6.1 General

Contract review ensures that customer enquiries and contract information are reviewed to identify the precise scope of work and resolve any problems associated with complying with customer requirements.

Customer enquiries requiring documented quotations are received as follows:

(a) Public advertising of the tender
(b) Written enquiries

(c) Telephone enquiries
(d) Personal enquiries
(e) Response to company advertising/marketing

6.2 Tender Review

6.2.1 Review of the Tender/Enquiry

The sales and marketing manager shall review the initial enquiry and ensure that all requirements of the customer are adequately defined and documented.

In this respect, the sales and marketing manager checks for the following requirements:

(a) Scope of work
(b) Customer specifications and associated documents
(c) Referenced standards, codes and statutory requirements
(d) Quality plan requirements
(e) Resources, facilities and personnel required
(f) Special training requirements
(g) Development of specialised equipment
(h) Costing
(i) Confidentiality aspects
(j) Documentation control
(k) Industrial/site agreements
(l) Programming of work
(m) Commercial conditions
(n) Traceability
(o) Customer-supplied product including storage and preservation requirements

The requirements of the enquiry and any problems associated with complying with the requirements are to be identified and resolved with the customer by the sales and marketing manager.

All correspondence and records of telephone discussions shall be entered in the quotation file.

6.2.2 Approving the Tender Submission

The sales and marketing manager shall prepare the tender bid or quotation for approval by the managing director.

6.2.3 Questionnaires

All queries regarding aspects of the quality system shall be referred to the quality manager prior to submission.

6.3 Contract Review

6.3.1 Comparison of Tender and Contract

If the tender/quotation is successful, the sales and marketing manager shall take the following action:

(a) The scope of the work contained in the order is to be compared with that in the tender/quotation and any variations recorded.
(b) Availability of facilities and personnel is to be confirmed, with any potential problems being recorded.
(c) The aspects covered in section 6.2.1 should be reviewed to confirm requirements.
(d) Commercial conditions (including costing) of the contract/order are to be checked against those in the tender/quotation.

Upon completion of all the above checks, and clarifications/resolution of outstanding areas with the customer, the sales and marketing manager shall open a job file which shall include all the pre- and post-award communications. The job file shall be identified by a unique job number as defined in QP.07.

6.3.2 Settling Queries

Should negotiation and resolution of variations with the customer be necessary prior to accepting an order, details of all relevant matters shall be formally submitted in writing to the customer for approval.

6.3.3 Telephone/Verbal Orders

In the event that a telephone or verbal enquiry/order is received and the customer does not intend to confirm the order in writing, the sales and marketing manager shall record the scope of work in sufficient detail and read the information back to the customer as an understanding of specified requirements. Where this type of contract is accepted by the company then acknowledgment automatically confirms the ability and capability to complete the work.

Note: Contracts of this nature should always be acknowledged in writing using the following format: "With reference to your recent enquiry our understanding of the workscope is as follows ... We shall proceed on that understanding unless advised otherwise."

6.4 Project Quality Plans

A project quality plan may be:

(a) a requirement of the specific contract;
(b) considered to be desirable given the scope of the contract.

The quality manager shall be responsible for collating the specific project quality plan which is made up of a project quality policy manual, project related procedures and where appropriate, inspection and test plans as defined in QP.09B.

The project quality plan shall be reviewed and approved by the managing director.

6.5 Change Orders

Change orders received from the customer are processed by the sales and marketing manager in accordance with 6.2 and 6.3 of this quality system procedure. Should the change impact on other operations, then a review meeting may need to be convened.

6.6 Records

Records of tender and contract review shall be maintained in the appropriate job file.

ABC COMPANY

QUALITY SYSTEM PROCEDURE
FOR

DOCUMENT CONTROL

DOCUMENT NO.: QP.04

	NAME	SIGNATURE	DATE
PREPARED BY:			
APPROVED BY:			

Copy no.: ______________

Controlled ( )

Uncontrolled ( )

TABLE OF CONTENTS

ISSUE HISTORY

ISSUE NO.	DATE	DESCRIPTION	REVISED BY	APPROVED BY
A	10 August 1993	Issued		

1.0 PURPOSE

The purposes of this procedure are:

- to establish and maintain a system to control all documents and data that relate to the company's quality system;
- to ensure that all quality-related documents are reviewed and approved for adequacy and that only the latest versions are available at all points of use.

2.0 SCOPE

This quality system procedure shall apply to all quality-related documents processed by ABC Company's personnel.

3.0 DEFINITIONS

3.1 Quality-related Documents

Quality-related documents are those documents defined within the quality system, i.e. quality system procedures, quality policy manual, work procedures, job descriptions, drawings, technical specifications, proformas and standards.

3.2 Senior Personnel

Line management reporting directly to the managing director.

4.0 REFERENCE MATERIAL

QP.01 – Writing Quality System and Work Procedures
QP.08 – Process Control

5.0 RESPONSIBILITIES

5.1 Managing Director

The managing director is responsible for:

(a) the preparation and revision of job descriptions;

(b) the approval of quality system procedures.

5.2 Quality Manager

The quality manager shall be responsible for:

(a) preparation and control of the quality policy manual and revisions/re-issues;
(b) preparation and control of quality system procedures and re-issues;
(c) holding a copy of all quality system procedures;
(d) maintenance and control of standards.

5.3 Senior Personnel

Senior personnel shall be responsible for:

(a) preparation and control of work procedures and re-issues;
(b) preparation and control of drawings and specifications.

5.4 Document Controller

The document controller shall issue documents that are to be distributed, at the request of the managing director, quality manager or senior personnel, as further defined in this quality system procedure. The document controller shall maintain the master document register. The document controller is responsible for removing or monitoring the destruction of obsolete documents from the point of use or for clearly marking documents which have been superseded.

6.0 PROCEDURE

6.1 Copy Control System

6.1.1 General

Distribution of quality-related documents within the company shall be managed so that the number of copies, and their whereabouts, are known. The extent of, and responsibility for, control are dependent on the type of document and extent of distribution.

6.1.2 Quality Policy Manual, Quality System Procedures and Work Procedures

These documents:

(a) have an extended and variable distribution;
(b) are updated by the quality manager or a responsible person as applicable;
(c) shall be distributed on a controlled copy basis by the document controller and hence shall be given:

- a copy number (see 6.1.2.1 of this section);
- a controlled/uncontrolled copy indicator.

The two indicators shall be located on the title page (page 1) in the following fashion:

Copy no.: ______________
Controlled ( )
Uncontrolled ( )

Alternatively an appropriate stamp may be employed to indicate controlled status and copy number.

6.1.2.1 Copy number Each copy of a quality-related document (see 6.1.2) shall be given a copy number, which shall commence at 1 and carry on 2, 3, 4 with each subsequent copy.

The copy numbers shall be controlled by the document controller via the document distribution register (see section 6.2).

6.1.2.2 Controlled/Uncontrolled The responsible person shall decide whether a copy shall be controlled or uncontrolled and advise the document controller accordingly.

Controlled copies:

(a) are subject to automatic revision servicing;
(b) have an "X" placed in the brackets on the title page indicating a controlled copy, i.e.: Controlled (X) or may be indicated as controlled by way of a red "controlled copy" stamp.

Unless specified, copies given to external suppliers and customers should be on an uncontrolled basis.

6.1.3 Job-related Documentation

These documents (e.g. drawings and technical specifications):

(a) have a limited and variable distribution;
(b) are monitored by the production manager;
(c) may be related to a specific job number in which case they shall be controlled through the job file.

Some documents (including those externally supplied to ABC Company) may be registered and distributed as defined in 6.1.2, if deemed necessary by the production manager.

6.2 Document Control Registers

6.2.1 Responsibility for Maintenance

The master document register shall be maintained by the document controller (see Appendix 1 of this procedure) and shall be completed for each document to be controlled, except as defined in 6.1.3.

The distribution register is maintained to register controlled copy holders of all documents (see Appendix 2 of the procedure).

6.2.2 Format

6.2.2.1 The master document register consists of the following information:

- Document Type – which describes the type of document being controlled which may be either quality policy manual, quality system procedures, work procedures, job descriptions, quality plans, standards and other applicable categories.
- Document Number – the unique identification number which relates directly to the document (e.g. quality system procedure number, work procedure number).
- Title – which describes the document name.
- Issue/Date – which is the document issue identifier commencing with A and progressing alphabetically. The issue date should also be included following a diagonal line in the appropriate box.

Note: Revisions of individual pages as required for the quality policy manual are registered in the "Revisions Page" of the document itself.

6.2.2.2 The distribution register consists of the following information:

- Document Number – which is a uniquely identifiable number which relates directly to the document (e.g. quality system procedure number, work procedure number).
- Issue – the issue identifier of the document.
- Document Title – which nominates the name of the document.
- Copy Number – which shall commence at "1" and continue 2, 3, 4, etc. This number shall be entered onto the title page (copy number) of the applicable document.
- Issued To – which is the name or title of the person to whom the document was issued.
- Acknowledgment – which shall record the receipt by the holder of the controlled document (or document controller) by way of initials.

6.3 Transmittal Note

6.3.1 Responsibilities of the Document Controller

The transmittal note (see Appendix 3 of this procedure) may be used to herald the dispatch of a document to an external party, and as a means by which, receipt can be confirmed. The document controller shall:

(a) number the transmittal note;
(b) complete the details on the transmittal note and forward it with a copy of the document;
(c) monitor the return of the signed notes to ensure that all copies have been received, obsolete documents have been removed and complete the acknowledgment section of the distribution register;
(d) when advised by senior personnel, clearly stamp obsolete documents with a "superseded" stamp where a document is still required at its point of issue.

6.3.2 Responsibilities of the Recipient

On the arrival of the transmittal note and document, the recipient should:

(a) sign the transmittal note;
(b) remove and destroy the obsolete document (if applicable) and replace with the new or if appropriate make the document available for "superseded" stamping;
(c) return the signed transmittal note to the document controller;
(d) advise the document controller if further copies are required to ensure the document is available at the point of use;
(e) review the document and ensure that all references nominated in the document are also available at the point of use.

Note: Internally distributed documents should be hand delivered or may be distributed using transmittal notes.

6.4 Hand-delivered Documents

If documents are hand delivered by the document controller, the recipient may sign the distribution register in the column provided to acknowledge receipt of a document and suitable disposal of the superseded document if applicable.

6.5 Review and Approval of Quality System Procedures

The system for review and approval of quality system and work procedures is described in QP.01.

6.6 Review and Approval of Other Quality-related Documents

All documents generated by ABC Co. are endorsed as "Approved By" to signify the managing director or senior personnel's review and approval of the documents.

Any amendments to these documents are returned to the originator for review as well as the approval of the managing director or senior personnel as applicable.

Externally generated documents such as standards and customer-supplied drawings shall be reviewed by any appropriately qualified senior personnel. Approval for use (i.e. adequacy of the document) shall be signified by endorsement on the document or accompanying transmittal as appropriate.

6.7 National Standards

National codes and standards are registered by the document controller and maintained in a central library. The quality manager is responsible for monitoring amendments and re-issues of standards on a regular basis, to ensure that obsolete documents are removed from use.

6.8 Contract Document Preparation

Contract documentation developed by the company (e.g. drawings and specifications) are prepared under the supervision of the production manager. The production manager shall nominate a document originator and prepare a brief to detail requirements. The production manager shall review said documents to verify internal requirements have been met, prior to submitting to the managing director for approval. Following approval, the document controller shall register the document prior to issue to the parties nominated by the production manager.

6.9 Forms

Master proformas are given individual form numbers and version numbers. These are controlled via the master document register, listing out all the terms which are in use within the company. Form numbers may take any uniquely registered number, but should wherever possible be related to any "parent" procedure to which it is associated. The first version of any form is issued as Version 1.

APPENDIXES

1. Master Document Register (QP.04.01)
2. Distribution Register (QP.04.02)
3. Transmittal Note (QP.04.03)

APPENDIX 1

MASTER DOCUMENT REGISTER

DOCUMENT TYPE:

DOCUMENT NO.	TITLE	ISSUE/DATE						

QP.04.01 Version 1

APPENDIX 2

DISTRIBUTION REGISTER

Document number: ______________________________ Issue: __________

Document title: ____

____

COPY NUMBER	ISSUED TO	ACKNOWLEDGMENT

QP.04.02 Version 1

APPENDIX 3

TRANSMITTAL NOTE		
To: ______________________ Attention: ______________________		Transmittal no.:
From:	Date:	Page of
Please find enclosed:		
Sent to you for information/comment/approval/other:		
Comments:		
Received:		Date:
Please sign and return this transmittal note to sender as evidence of receipt.		

QP.04.03 Version 1

ABC COMPANY

QUALITY SYSTEM PROCEDURE

FOR

PURCHASING

DOCUMENT NO.: QP.05

	NAME	SIGNATURE	DATE
PREPARED BY:			
APPROVED BY:			

Copy no.: ______________

Controlled ( )

Uncontrolled ( )

TABLE OF CONTENTS

ISSUE HISTORY

ISSUE NO.	DATE	DESCRIPTION	REVISED BY	APPROVED BY
A	23 August 1993	Issued		

1.0 PURPOSE

The purposes of this procedure are:

- to ensure that all ABC Company's suppliers are evaluated and have the ability and capacity to meet both the customer's and company's requirements prior to engagement;
- to ensure that all ABC Company's purchasing documents adequately describe the product or service being purchased.

2.0 SCOPE

This procedure applies to goods and services purchased by ABC Company.

This procedure does not apply to the purchase of "non-contract related" goods, e.g. stationery.

3.0 DEFINITIONS

3.1 Purchase Requisition

A document (including drawings and specifications) which clearly describes the scope of works being purchased.

4.0 REFERENCE MATERIAL

QP.02 – Management Review
QP.09A – Receiving Inspection and Testing
QP.07 – Identification and Traceability

5.0 RESPONSIBILITIES

5.1 Managing Director

The managing director is responsible for co-ordinating the evaluation and approval of suppliers and subcontractors for the approved suppliers list.

5.2 Quality Manager

The quality manager is responsible for the assessment (by audit) of potential new suppliers if required.

5.3 Production Manager

The production manager shall prepare purchase requisitions as required.

5.4 Purchasing Officer

The purchasing officer has a responsibility to:

(a) approve purchase requisitions, prepare purchase orders and place them with approved suppliers;
(b) maintain the approved supplier list and records files;
(c) prepare and issue questionnaires, review responses and approve suppliers;
(d) summarise supplier performance for management consideration (see QP.02).

5.5 Production Manager

The production manager shall allocate a job number (see QP.07).

6.0 PROCEDURE

6.1 Suppliers

Only suppliers who are listed on the approved suppliers list shall be used for the procurement of contract goods and services.

6.1.1 Evaluation

Evaluation and approval of suppliers shall be determined by any or all of the following methods, depending on the nature and extent of the goods or services to be purchased:

(a) Assessment (audit) of the supplier's organisation by a site visit, to verify quality system and process controls.

(b) Use of a third party approval service, such as a recognised and accredited certifying body to confirm product or company certification.
(c) Continual verification through incoming inspection (see QP.09A).
(d) Records of the supplier's previously demonstrated capability.
(e) Supplier questionnaire to address specific requirements of the purchased item or service. The questionnaire shall be completed by interview or telephone survey.

The type of evaluation or approval applied to each supplier shall be outlined on the approved suppliers list (see Appendix 1) against that supplier.

Suitable records (e.g. audit reports, inspection reports, receipt inspections, reports from third party auditors, questionnaires) detailing the evidence of evaluation for each supplier shall be retained by the purchasing officer.

Notes:

1. Where the purchasing officer considers purchases have a minor impact on the final item and supplies are abundant, then a percentage incoming inspection may be carried out as the basis for assessment.
2. In the case of a monopoly supplier, proprietary items or licensee arrangements, no assessment is undertaken; however, ongoing review and receiving inspection is still carried out.

6.1.2 Approval and Ongoing Review

Following a successful evaluation, the successful supplier shall be placed on the approved suppliers list.

A supplier's performance shall be re-evaluated during management review in accordance with QP.02 on an ongoing basis to ensure that the supplier continues to comply with the company's purchasing and quality requirements.

Where late or defective goods or services are received, action shall be taken to record the problem and the purchasing officer shall address the matter with the supplier (see QP.09A).

Where the matter is unresolved, in that the supplier continues to supply late or defective items or is unwilling to make efforts to improve performance, the approved suppliers list shall be annotated to indicate that the supplier is not to be used, or that conditions apply to his use.

6.2 Purchasing

6.2.1 Purchase Requisition

All contract-related purchases shall be initiated by the raising of a purchase requisition.

Purchase requisitions shall be clearly and concisely written and include all applicable requirements, including those specified by the customer's contract, order, or company policy. This may include details such as:

(a) the type, class, grade, style, or other precise identification;
(b) the title, number, and issue of the quality system standard to be applied;
(c) test certificates, delivery dates, packing and shipping instructions;
(d) appropriate drawings, processes, inspection instructions, and special instructions;
(e) any requirements for approval and/or qualification of product, procedures, process equipment or personnel;
(f) the job number which shall be suffixed to the requisition number.

The requisition shall be prepared by the production manager and approved and reviewed prior to processing by the purchasing officer. Order values in excess of the value from time to time specified shall be authorised by the managing director prior to forwarding to the purchasing officer.

6.2.2 Purchase Order

All details on the purchase requisition shall be transferred to the purchase order. If supply is not available from an approved supplier, alternative sources of supply shall be evaluated and approved by the purchasing officer prior to placing of the order.

Should the customer's contract, order or company policy require verification of goods or services at source, the purchase order must include a statement to the effect that will allow the company or customer access to the supplier's premises for that verification. Purchase orders shall be authorised by either the purchasing officer or the managing director after ensuring that the purchase order accurately reflects the requirements of the approved requisition, prior to issuing to the supplier.

6.2.3 Purchase Order Distribution

Purchase orders are distributed as follows:

(a) Original – Supplier
(b) One copy – Stores (for use in receiving inspection)
(c) One copy – Retained in book (for administration and accounts)
(d) One copy – Job file (optional)

6.3 Verification of Purchased Products

Where specified in a contract, the customer or his representative shall be allowed to verify that the company's products conform to specified requirements either through:

(a) inspection at ABC Company's premises;
(b) inspection on receipt;
(c) inspection at the sub-supplier's premises.

All such inspections should be arranged by the customer through the quality manager.

Inspection and acceptance of work by the customer does not exonerate ABC Company of its responsibility to provide acceptable products as stipulated in the quality system and/or contract requirements nor does it preclude subsequent rejection of the quality of products by the customer.

Should the customer elect to carry out verification at the subcontractor's premises, such verification shall not be used by ABC Company as effective control of quality by the subcontractor (see section 6.1.1).

APPENDIXES

1. Approved Suppliers List (QP.05.01)
2. Purchase Requisition (QP.05.02)
3. Purchase Order (QP.05.03)

APPENDIX 1

APPROVED SUPPLIERS LIST

COMPANY NAME	ADDRESS	PHONE & FAX NO.	PRODUCT/SERVICE SUPPLIED	ASSESSMENT TYPE

Approved: ______________________ Date: ______________________

QP.05.01 Version 1

APPENDIX 2

ABC COMPANY PTY LTD

PURCHASE REQUISITION

Requisition no.:

Date:

Preferred supplier:
(if known)

Required by: ________________

Deliver to: ________________

Job no.: ________________

ITEM	QUANTITY	DETAILED DESCRIPTION	ITEM COST (if known)

Prepared by: ________________ Date: ________________ Order no. allocated:

Approved by: ________________ Date: ________________ ________________

Distribution: White – Purchasing officer Pink – Originator

QP.05.02 Version 1

APPENDIX 3

ABC COMPANY
PTY LTD

123 Iso St.
Widgitsville

Tel: (09) 123 2334
Facsimile: (09) 123 2333

Note: All deliveries to be sent to the above address.

PURCHASE ORDER

Supplier:

Order no.:

Date:

Packaging, delivery dockets report and invoices must include the job number.

Date required:

ITEM	QUANTITY	DETAILED DESCRIPTION	ITEM COST
Authorised by:		Date: **TOTAL**	

Distribution: White – Supplier Pink – Stores Yellow – Job file Blue – Fixed in book

QP.05.03 Version 1

ABC COMPANY

QUALITY SYSTEM PROCEDURE

FOR

PURCHASER-SUPPLIED PRODUCT

DOCUMENT NO.: QP.06

	NAME	SIGNATURE	DATE
PREPARED BY:			
APPROVED BY:			

Copy no.: __________

Controlled ( )

Uncontrolled ( )

TABLE OF CONTENTS

ISSUE HISTORY

ISSUE NO.	DATE	DESCRIPTION	REVISED BY	APPROVED BY
A	10 August 1993	Issued		

1.0 PURPOSE

The purposes of this procedure are:

- to ensure that products supplied by the customer are verified, stored, and maintained in a suitable condition ready for incorporation into the manufacturing process;
- to ensure that any purchaser-supplied product which is lost, damaged or unsuitable for use is reported to the customer.

2.0 SCOPE

This procedure applies to all products and services supplied by the customer, for incorporation into an order placed with ABC Company.

3.0 DEFINITIONS

3.1 Purchaser-supplied (Customer-supplied) Product

Any material, product, service, or equipment which is supplied to ABC Company by the customer for use on a specific contract, sometimes referred to as "free issue material".

4.0 REFERENCE MATERIAL

QP.03 – Contract Review
QP.05 – Purchasing
QP.09A – Receiving Inspection and Testing
QP.13 – Handling, Storage, Packaging and Delivery

5.0 RESPONSIBILITIES

5.1 Sales and Marketing Manager

The sales and marketing manager is responsible for issuing to stores a "dummy" purchase order for all products supplied by the customer.

5.2 Production Manager

The production manager is responsible for:

(a) inspecting all customer-supplied products;
(b) reporting any lost or damaged customer-supplied materials, products and equipment to the customer;
(c) determining the suitability of product and reporting any anomalies to the customer.

5.3 Storeman

The storeman is responsible for:

(a) verifying that the product delivered matches the accompanying documentation;
(b) handling and storing products, components, etc., supplied by the customer in a manner which prevents undue damage or deterioration;
(c) recording all special customer requirements for handling, storage and delivery in the job file.

6.0 PROCEDURE

6.1 During a tender/contract review (see QP.03), the sales and marketing manager shall identify all products which are being supplied by the customer. A list of products shall be placed on the job file and a copy shall be issued to the stores on a dummy purchase order. The dummy purchase order shall be clearly marked "free issue item" and be sufficiently detailed with description and delivery date, as defined in QP.05.

6.2 Customer-supplied materials or products will be treated in exactly the same way as ABC Company's purchased products and will be verified to ensure it is suitable for use so as not to affect the quality of work produced by ABC Company.

6.3 All incoming customer-supplied materials and products shall be inspected upon receipt by the production manager and the storeman in accordance with procedure QP.09A to ensure it is:

(a) properly identified and in accordance with accompanying documentation and the dummy purchase order;
(b) undamaged and complete.

The storeman shall identify the material or product with the appropriate job number.

Any customer-supplied materials and products which is lost, damaged or not received by the nominated delivery date shall be recorded in the appropriate job file, and reported to the customer in writing by the production manager.

6.4 The production manager shall evaluate purchaser-supplied product to ensure its suitability for incorporation into the works. Any unsuitable or doubtful materials or products shall be reported to the customer in writing.

6.5 Storage

All customer-supplied materials and products shall be stored in a way to prevent deterioration and damage (see QP.13) or in the manner specified and noted during contract review (see QP.03).

ABC COMPANY

QUALITY SYSTEM PROCEDURE

FOR

PRODUCT IDENTIFICATION AND TRACEABILITY

DOCUMENT NO.: QP.07

	NAME	SIGNATURE	DATE
PREPARED BY:			
APPROVED BY:			

Copy no.: ____________

Controlled ( )

Uncontrolled ( )

TABLE OF CONTENTS

ISSUE HISTORY

ISSUE NO.	DATE	DESCRIPTION	REVISED BY	APPROVED BY
A	10 August 1993	Issued		

1.0 PURPOSE

To maintain a system which provides identification and where contractually required, traceability of all products manufactured by ABC Company.

2.0 SCOPE

This quality system procedure applies to all records, goods and documentation associated with each order and where specified by the customer, traceable to the extent required.

3.0 DEFINITIONS

3.1 Product Identification

The system or method used to link all manufactured goods, records and other documentation associated with each job.

3.2 Traceability

The method which allows a product to be traced from a point in its origin to a later point through documentation.

3.3 Job Number

The unique identifying number allocated to each order or contract.

4.0 REFERENCE MATERIAL

QP.06 – Purchaser-supplied Product
QP.09 – Inspection and Testing
QP.14 – Quality Records

5.0 RESPONSIBILITIES

5.1 Production Manager

The production manager is responsible for:

(a) ensuring that job numbers are issued and used;
(b) ensuring that product identification is maintained at all stages of manufacture;
(c) ensuring that purchased material is correctly identified.

6.0 PROCEDURE

All manufactured goods, purchaser-supplied products and associated documentation shall be identified with a unique job number wherever practicable.

Purchased products are identified with the appropriate job number, if they are bought for a specific contract.

6.1 Job Number Register

The production manager shall maintain a register of job numbers. Details recorded in the register shall include, but are not limited to:

(a) job number;
(b) customer's name and contact name;
(c) customer's order number for the job;
(d) description of work (reference to drawing numbers, etc.);
(e) date initiated;
(f) date of completion (shipment).

6.2 Identification

6.2.1 Purchased Material

All incoming raw materials shall be inspected upon receipt to ensure they are properly identified to the accompanying documentation (see QP.09).

The purchased items or their container shall be identified with the order number which includes the nominated job number if the items have been purchased for a specific contract.

6.2.2 Purchaser-supplied Material

All products supplied by the customer in accordance with procedure QP.06 shall, wherever practicable, be identified with the appropriate job number upon receipt after checking against the dummy order number.

6.2.3 Manufactured Goods

Wherever practicable, all goods shall be identified during handling and storage through the job number. All samples, or batches of goods, shall be identified by means of labels or markings, highlighting the ABC Co.'s job number.

Multiple numbers (batches) of goods may be collectively identified (e.g. via pallets or shelves).

6.2.4 Records

All records and documentation associated with the order shall be identified and filed via the job number (see QP.14).

6.3 Traceability

Where traceability has been specified and clarified at contract review, the production manager shall prepare a contract specific work procedure for each specific item requiring traceability records. The records shall be maintained in the job file in a folder clearly marked "traceability data".

ABC COMPANY

QUALITY SYSTEM PROCEDURE

FOR

PROCESS CONTROL

DOCUMENT NO.: QP.08

	NAME	SIGNATURE	DATE
PREPARED BY:			
APPROVED BY:			

Copy no.: ____________

Controlled ( )

Uncontrolled ( )

TABLE OF CONTENTS

ISSUE HISTORY

ISSUE NO.	DATE	DESCRIPTION	REVISED BY	APPROVED BY
A	10 August 1993	Issued		

1.0 PURPOSE

The purpose of this quality system procedure is to provide a method for ensuring that processes which directly affect quality are planned and carried out under controlled conditions.

2.0 SCOPE

This quality system procedure applies to all operations which affect the quality of ABC Company's manufacturing activity.

3.0 DEFINITIONS

Nil

4.0 REFERENCE MATERIAL

QP.01 – Writing Quality System and Work Procedures
QP.03 – Contract Review
QP.04 – Document Control
QP.09B – In-process and Final Inspection and Testing
QP.16 – Training
QP.17 – Statistical Process Monitoring

5.0 RESPONSIBILITIES

5.1 Production Manager

The production manager is responsible for:

(a) identifying the need for, and providing, adequate written work procedures for the operation of equipment or performance of duties to the appropriate employees;
(b) planning production processes using inspection and test plans or quality plans where required;
(c) monitoring the standards of workmanship of employees;
(d) identifying and controlling special processes;

(e) identifying the need for and providing adequate work procedures for the preventive maintenance of equipment and machinery which can affect quality or delivery schedules.

6.0 PROCEDURE

6.1 Planning

The production manager shall plan production using contract documents.

Where an inspection and test plan (ITP) or quality plan is identified as being required at contract review stage (see QP.09B and QP.03 respectively), the production manager, in conjunction with the quality manager shall be responsible for preparing these documents.

Quality plans or ITPs form part of the job file and are distributed to employees involved for information.

ITPs shall detail all critical process activities including the approvals of processing equipment and personnel and shall ensure compliance with specified requirements.

The production manager is responsible for ensuring that all nominated inspections and tests are carried out and that the ITP is progressively signed off as further defined in QP.09B.

Quality plans and ITPs are issued and maintained as controlled documents (see QP.04).

6.2 Work Procedures

6.2.1 Scope

Documented procedures or work procedures (see QP.01) shall be provided by the production manager, to provide written directions and instructions to personnel covering all work and/or workmanship criteria that directly affect the quality of finished work.

Work procedures shall be prepared by the production manager or his nominee, using the knowledge and expertise of all personnel associated with the particular kind of work.

The documented work procedures written by ABC Company personnel shall be prepared indicating approval of the method and equipment to be used for control of the process.

The production manager shall ensure that his subordinates use the appropriate work procedures provided, by continual monitoring of processes. He shall also ensure the practical effectiveness of work procedures as documented.

Work procedures are issued and maintained as controlled documents (see QP.04).

6.2.2 Format

The work procedures shall nominate why and how a task is to be performed, the equipment to be used and prerequisite skills that may be required. The written instruction shall include (as applicable):

(a) specific standards, codes, statutory or customer requirements;
(b) the required quality of workmanship (i.e. acceptance criteria);
(c) appropriate drawings, sketches, and flow charts to assist the operator in interpretation of the instruction;
(d) specific aspects of operator or public safety which may need to be considered;
(e) appropriate reference to a specific contract or job;
(f) the operating environment required for both operator and equipment;
(g) equipment to be used to perform the task, and qualification of processes or equipment necessary.

6.3 Criteria for Workmanship

The acceptance criteria for workmanship may include, but is not limited to:

(a) the presentation of finished goods;
(b) reference to national codes and standards;
(c) the timeliness of delivery;
(d) allowable tolerances.

6.4 Special Processes

The following list identifies the special processes carried out by ABC Company:

(a) Welding
(b) Painting

Welding processes shall be performed by qualified welding personnel using qualified welding procedures and controlled equipment.

The training details and applicable qualifications for personnel carrying out special processes shall be recorded (see QP.16) and made available for verification by the customer's representative as required.

Painting is carried out in accordance with paint suppliers' data sheets which represent the qualified method of application. Such data sheets are retained as controlled documents, unless specified on the labels of paint tins, etc.

6.5 Process Monitoring

The effectiveness of the manufacturing process is monitored by the quality manager (see QP.17).

APPENDIX

1. Work Procedure Form (QP.01.01)

APPENDIX 1

WORK PROCEDURE	No.: Page:	Issue: of
Title: Equipment/Materials:		

OPERATIONS	
NO.	DESCRIPTION

Controlled (   )

Copy no. ______   Prepared by: ____________   Date: ____________

Uncontrolled (   )   Approved by: ____________   Date: ____________

QP.01.01 Version 1

ABC COMPANY

QUALITY SYSTEM PROCEDURE

FOR

RECEIVING INSPECTION AND TESTING

DOCUMENT NO.: QP.09A

	NAME	SIGNATURE	DATE
PREPARED BY:			
APPROVED BY:			

Copy no.: ____________

Controlled ( )

Uncontrolled ( )

TABLE OF CONTENTS

ISSUE HISTORY

ISSUE NO.	DATE	DESCRIPTION	REVISED BY	APPROVED BY
A	10 August 1993	Issued		

1.0 PURPOSE

The purpose of this quality system procedure is to ensure that incoming material and products are inspected and/or tested for conformance to specified requirements, prior to use.

2.0 SCOPE

This quality system procedure applies to all incoming goods that are purchased in order to fulfil contract requirements (e.g. to be incorporated into ABC Company's product or work carried out on behalf of customers). It does not apply to non-contract related goods (e.g. stationery).

3.0 DEFINITIONS

Nil

4.0 REFERENCE MATERIAL

QP.05 – Purchasing
QP.07 – Product Identification and Traceability
QP.14 – Quality Records

5.0 RESPONSIBILITIES

5.1 Storeman

The storeman shall be responsible for performing receiving inspection on all incoming goods.

5.2 Purchasing Officer

The purchasing officer is responsible for the verification of unacceptable deliveries prior to the issue of a defect advice note to the appropriate supplier.

6.0 PROCEDURE

6.1 Receiving Inspection and Testing

All material supplied in accordance with a purchase order shall be inspected by the storeman upon receipt for damage, completeness and identification, as specified on the purchase order documents (see QP.05).

Incoming material shall remain in the "Receiving Stores" area, and should be withheld from use pending completion of receiving inspection and/or testing or receipt of documentation (e.g. material certificates).

Should release of material be required prior to this, it may only be done when the identification and use of the purchased material is traceable to its end use and under the instruction of the production manager. Hence, if required, traceability shall ensure that the material and all end products in which it was used may be recalled if the material is found to be inadequate.

Acceptance of the supplied material shall be indicated by signing and dating the appropriate delivery documentation and stores copy of the purchase order and removal from the "Receiving store" area.

The delivery documentation and stores copy of the purchase order shall be forwarded to accounts for payment and then to the job file.

Accepted incoming goods are physically marked or tagged with the job number when purchased for a particular contract (see QP.07).

Any damaged item, missing item, or incorrect identification from the delivery docket or invoice shall be:

(a) marked on the carrier's copy of delivery docket;
(b) documented by the storeman onto a defect advice note.

Material which is damaged shall remain in the designated holding area, and shall be clearly marked or labelled until the purchasing officer has resolved the matter with the supplier.

The defect advice note shall be forwarded by the purchasing officer to the supplier and a copy of the note attached to the supplier's history file.

6.2 Receiving Inspection and Testing Records

All inspection and test records delivered with the material and the signed stores copy of the purchase order shall be retained as quality records.

Records shall be stored by the production manager on the job file and in a manner to prevent damage or deterioration as required by procedure QP.14.

APPENDIX

1. Defect Advice Note (QP.09A.01)

APPENDIX 1

DEFECT ADVICE NOTE	No.:

Purchase order no.: ______________________ Job no.: ____________

Delivery docket/advice note no.: __________ Delivery date: __________

Supplier: ____

Material description: ______________________________________

____

Nature of defect: ____

____

____

____

Prepared by: ______________________ Date: ______________

With respect to the material(s) described above, the supplier is requested to: (Tick as applicable)

- replace the defective material(s) ☐
- collect the defective material(s) ☐
- issue credit note for defective material(s) ☐
- refund payments made for defective material(s) ☐
- Other (specify) ______________________________ ☐

  ____

Issued by: ____________________(Purchasing Officer) Date: __________

QP.09A.01 Version 1

ABC COMPANY

QUALITY SYSTEM PROCEDURE

FOR

IN-PROCESS AND FINAL INSPECTION AND TESTING

DOCUMENT NO.: QP.09B

	NAME	SIGNATURE	DATE
PREPARED BY:			
APPROVED BY:			

Copy no.: ______________

Controlled ( )

Uncontrolled ( )

TABLE OF CONTENTS

ISSUE HISTORY

ISSUE NO.	DATE	DESCRIPTION	REVISED BY	APPROVED BY
A	10 August 1993	Issued		

1.0 PURPOSE

The purpose of this procedure is to maintain a system which identifies and plans the various inspection and test stages required by ABC Company and/or the contract.

2.0 SCOPE

This procedure applies to all work carried out by ABC Company.

3.0 DEFINITIONS

Nil

4.0 REFERENCE MATERIAL

QP.11 – Nonconforming Product
QP.14 – Quality Records

5.0 RESPONSIBILITIES

5.1 Production Manager

The production manager is responsible for nominating the type and frequency of inspections and tests to be carried out on manufactured products.

5.2 QC Inspector

The QC inspector shall be responsible for performing in-process and final inspections at the direction of the production manager.

6.0 PROCEDURE

6.1 In-process Inspection and Testing

Where appropriate or specified, inspection and test plans (ITPs) or job cards shall be prepared by the production manager and reviewed/approved by the quality manager outlining the various activities contributing to the manufacture of a product. At each stage, any hold or verification point shall be nominated on the ITP, together with required acceptance criteria and reference documentation. Products shall not progress to the next stage of production until all nominated in-process inspections and tests have been performed by the nominated QC inspector. Any nonconforming products shall be handled in accordance with procedure QP.11.

The ITP shall be prepared by breaking down each production activity in a step-by-step process. Each activity will then be analysed for inspections and tests that may be required prior to proceeding to the next stage (see Appendix 1).

Evidence of inspection status shall be annotated onto the ITP by the QC inspector or customer inspector as applicable by signing each hold, witness or inspection stage after successful completion.

6.2 Final Inspection and Testing

Completed batches shall be inspected and tested using the final inspection and test checklist (see Appendix 2). This function shall be performed by the production manager or his nominated QC inspector.

The final inspection and test shall include an overview of the whole process to ensure that all in-process inspections and tests have been satisfactorily completed and passed and that all documentation is complete.

6.3 Inspection and Test Records

Inspection and test records form part of the quality records.

Records shall be stored by the production manager on the job file in a manner to prevent damage or deterioration as required by procedure QP.14.

APPENDIXES

1. Inspection and Test Plan (QP.09B.01)
2. Final Inspection and Test Checklist (QP.09B.02)

APPENDIX 1

INSPECTION AND TEST PLAN

Customer: ____________ Job no.: ____________

Prepared by: ____________ Date: ____________ Page of Issue no.: ____________

ITEM	CHECK AND INSPECTIONS	APPLICABLE STANDARD/PROC.	ACCEPTANCE CRITERIA	INSPECTION BY		REMARKS
				ABC	CUSTOMER	

H = Hold (do not proceed) W = Witness (present at test) I = Inspect/test R = Record or review documents

QP.09B.01 Version 1

APPENDIX 2

FINAL INSPECTION AND TEST CHECKLIST		
Customer: ______		
Job no.: ______ Order/Contract no.: ______		
Date of inspection/test: ______		
Description: ______		
PARAMETER	**CHECK (Y/N)**	**REMARKS**
All in-process inspections and tests completed as necessary?		
All client inspections and tests nominated in the order completed?		
Nonconforming items dispositioned and closed out?		
All records completed and collated?		
All packaging and preservation in accordance with requirements?		
General remarks:		
This order is approved for release	Yes ☐	No ☐
Signed: ______	Date: ______	

QP.09B.02 Version 1

ABC COMPANY

QUALITY SYSTEM PROCEDURE

FOR

INSPECTION, MEASURING AND TEST EQUIPMENT

DOCUMENT NO.: QP.10

	NAME	SIGNATURE	DATE
PREPARED BY:			
APPROVED BY:			

Copy no.: ____________

Controlled ( )

Uncontrolled ( )

TABLE OF CONTENTS

ISSUE HISTORY

ISSUE NO.	DATE	DESCRIPTION	REVISED BY	APPROVED BY
A	10 August 1993	Issued		

1.0 PURPOSE

The objective of this quality system procedure is to:

(a) maintain a system for controlling, calibrating, and maintaining all inspection, measuring and test equipment and devices to demonstrate the conformance of product to specified requirements;
(b) ensure that all equipment is of the correct type and range and has the necessary accuracy to verify conformance to the company's and customer's requirements.

2.0 SCOPE

This quality system procedure applies to all inspection, measuring and test equipment and devices used during manufacturing which are owned by the company, provided by an outside supplier, owned by individuals or customer supplied.

3.0 DEFINITIONS

3.1 Calibration

A comparison of an instrument or measuring device against another instrument or device of which the accuracy is known and traceable to national or international standards.

3.2 National Standard

The national standard of measurement held within each country.

3.3 National Codes and Standards

Documented requirements relating to standardised practices.

3.4 Reference Standard

A standard which has been externally calibrated against, or traceable to, a national standard.

3.5 Working Standard

Standards which are calibrated against the reference standard and used in everyday work.

4.0 REFERENCE MATERIAL

QP.16 – Training

5.0 RESPONSIBILITIES

5.1 Production Manager

The production manager shall:

- ensure that all personnel are suitably qualified and trained to use calibrated equipment;
- implement and maintain the calibration system for all inspection, measuring and test equipment;
- ensure that newly purchased measuring and test equipment is subjected to appropriate calibration within the company, or at an accredited laboratory as appropriate;
- ensure that scheduled inspection of measuring and test equipment is subjected to appropriate calibration within the company, or at an accredited laboratory, at the predetermined time;
- organise re-calibration or disposal of nonconforming or inadequate inspection, measuring and test equipment;
- ensure that inspection, measuring and test equipment are suitable for the intended use in association with the leading hand or QC inspector;
- ensure that subcontractor-used or customer-supplied equipment is suitable for the intended use;
- ensure that subcontractor-used or customer-supplied equipment is properly calibrated and maintained.

5.2 Leading Hand and QC Inspectors

Leading hand and QC inspectors shall:

- visually check all equipment prior to use to ensure that it is in a serviceable condition;
- ensure that equipment with an expired calibration life is removed from use and is re-calibrated or replaced prior to use.

6.0 PROCEDURE

6.1 General

Effective calibration of equipment and the correct use of that equipment ensures the validity of the results obtained. Calibration shall be performed in accordance with the "equipment calibration schedule" (see Appendix 1).

Calibration records are established and maintained to provide objective evidence that all inspection, measure and test equipment are effectively controlled. To this end, employee-owned inspection and measuring devices shall not be used on ABC Company's orders without being subjected to the requirements of this procedure.

6.2 Control of Inspection, Measuring and Test Equipment

6.2.1 Selection of Inspection, Measuring and Test Equipment

The technical requirements of the product shall be reviewed by the production manager or his nominee prior to the purchase of any new equipment. This review ensures that the selected equipment has the necessary measurement and testing capability, stability, and range compatible with the intended application.

Any design data supplied with, or used in the selection of, the equipment shall be retained by the production manager for the working life of the equipment.

Inspection, measuring and testing equipment design documents and/or manufacturer's brochures of the equipment shall be held by the production manager and made available to the customer's representative and other authorised personnel to demonstrate the adequacy and accuracy of the equipment.

6.2.2 Environmental Conditions

The environmental conditions of use for calibration, inspection, measurement and test shall be taken into consideration in the selection process.

The equipment selection process and conditions for ongoing use shall take into consideration recommended environmental conditions of use as made by:

(a) national codes and standards;
(b) manufacturer's recommendations;
(c) historical aspects.

6.2.3 Equipment Identification

All company equipment shall be identified by its unique allocated number which shall be known as the "equipment number". The unique number shall be cross referenced to the equipment serial number where one is available and shall be clearly marked on the equipment or its container.

The equipment record card (see Appendix 2) shall be used to register the equipment numbers.

6.2.4 Storage and Handling

All measuring, inspection and test equipment shall be cleaned and preserved as appropriate, returned to its container or packaging, and held in a suitable area to prevent damage, deterioration or change to dimensional or functional characteristics.

The storage and handling of measuring, inspection and test equipment shall be subject to the approval of the production manager.

6.3 Calibration

6.3.1 Equipment Calibration Schedule

All existing and newly acquired equipment (including purchaser supplied) shall be calibrated in accordance with the equipment calibration/service schedule (see Appendix 3).

This schedule lists:

1. equipment description;
2. equipment number;
3. calibration due date;
4. service due date.

6.3.2 Equipment/Calibration Record Cards

An equipment record card (see Appendix 2) and an equipment calibration/service record card (see Appendix 3) shall be maintained for each item of equipment calibrated. Details on the card include:

(a) equipment description, manufacturer, range and model/serial number;
(b) equipment number;
(c) calibration interval and calibration procedure;
(d) usual location;
(e) calibration date;
(f) calibration due date;
(g) calibration source;
(h) calibration certificate number;
(i) equipment error adjustment;
(j) calibration procedure and/or comments;
(k) service date;
(l) service due date;
(m) service contractor;
(n) remarks.

Equipment calibration/service record cards are reviewed quarterly by the production manager or his nominee to ensure timely recall of equipment scheduled for re-calibration or service.

6.3.3 Calibration Source

All inspection, measuring and test equipment shall be calibrated in accordance with the requirements of the manufacturer or national codes and standards.

Reference standards, where utilised, shall be certified by an accredited facility having standards traceable to "national standards", or to customer approved and documented alternative methods.

6.3.3.1 Internal Calibration Internal calibration is limited to checking working standards at intervals shown on the equipment calibration schedule in accordance with appropriate work procedures.

The calibrations are performed by suitably trained personnel (see QP.16). Details are recorded on the equipment calibration/service record card. The testing and approving officers sign and date the calibration record card under the "Remarks" column.

6.3.3.2 External Calibration External calibration is carried out by laboratories holding the relevant national accreditation. Company reference standards are subject to external calibration. A certificate of calibration is required.

6.3.4 Calibration Intervals

Calibration intervals are determined by the production manager in conjunction with standard requirements, manufacturer's recommendations, and the purpose and extent of use. Calibration intervals may be reviewed subject to intended use and calibration history.

6.3.5 Calibration Confirmation

All equipment should be labelled with a calibration sticker (see Appendix 4) which identifies the equipment number and the next calibration due date. This information is traceable to the equipment calibration/service record card and the equipment calibration schedule.

6.3.6 Nonconforming Equipment

Equipment that is either out of calibration life or defective shall be identified with a suitable tag or label where possible. The equipment shall not be used until it has been repaired and calibrated.

6.3.7 Sealing for Integrity

Adjustable equipment, which is fixed at one point, shall at the time of calibration, have a suitable integrity seal fixed to prevent adjustment.

The seal shall be affixed in a position which would destroy the seal if subsequent adjustment takes place.

Equipment with a broken integrity seal must be regarded as nonconforming and processed according to 6.3.6.

The production manager shall reference the requirement for an integrity seal on the equipment record card.

6.4 Faulty Equipment

Any equipment which has been involved in any event which may affect its accuracy must be recalibrated, regardless of the calibration life left before the next scheduled calibration date.

Items calibrated in accordance with the calibration schedule found to require adjustment or replacement shall be reviewed to determine the cause and future action. The production manager shall assess and document the validity of the work inspected with the equipment since the previous calibration. This assessment shall be documented.

If sufficient doubt exists regarding the validity of the previous tests, the production manager shall instigate a retest or recall of the previous work or test results.

6.5 Checks Before Use of Equipment

All equipment shall be checked prior to use. The check includes:

(a) calibration sticker, to confirm equipment number and within calibration life;
(b) integrity seal where applicable, to confirm equipment has not been adjusted since calibration;
(c) visual, to confirm equipment is serviceable and has not suffered damage;
(d) zero check where applicable, to confirm equipment has not deviated.

The equipment number of all inspection, measuring and test equipment (utilised for "on-the-job" tests, measurements, and inspections) shall be recorded.

6.6 Recall

The production manager shall ensure that test records include the equipment number, so that recalls due to faulty equipment may be accurately performed.

APPENDIXES

1. Equipment Calibration/Service Schedule (QP.10.01)
2. Equipment Record Card (QP.10.02)
3. Equipment Calibration/Service Record (QP.10.03)
4. Calibration Sticker

APPENDIX 1

EQUIPMENT CALIBRATION/SERVICE SCHEDULE

EQUIPMENT NUMBER	YEAR:											
	JAN	FEB	MAR	APR	MAY	JUN	JUL	AUG	SEP	OCT	NOV	DEC

"I" = Internal calibration "E" = External calibration "S" = Service

Approved: Date:

QP.10.01 Version 1

APPENDIX 2

EQUIPMENT RECORD CARD	
Equipment type: __________	Equipment number: __________
Model number: __________	Serial number: __________
Manufacturer: __________	
Agent: __________	
Address: __________	
__________	
Calibration interval (internal): __________	
(external): __________	
Calibration procedure: __________	
Calibration source/standard:	
Equipment range: __________	
Equipment error adjustment: __________	
Equipment location: __________	
External Calibration Authority	
Name of company: __________	
Address: __________	
__________	
Telephone: __________	Facsimile: __________
Contact names: __________	
Comments:	
Approved:	Date:

QP.10.02 Version 1

APPENDIX 3

EQUIPMENT CALIBRATION/SERVICE RECORD

EQUIPMENT NUMBER: EQUIPMENT TYPE:

DATE OF CALIBRATION OR SERVICE	INTERNAL/ EXTERNAL	CERTIFICATE NUMBER	REMARKS	CALIBRATION DUE DATE

QP.10.03 Version 1

APPENDIX 4

CALIBRATION STICKER

(Enlarged)

Equipment no.: ______________________________

Date calibrated: ______________________________

Cal. due date: ______________________________

Signed: ______________________________

ABC COMPANY

QUALITY SYSTEM PROCEDURE

FOR

CONTROL OF NONCONFORMING PRODUCT

DOCUMENT NO.: QP.11

	NAME	SIGNATURE	DATE
PREPARED BY:			
APPROVED BY:			

Copy no.: ______________

Controlled ( )

Uncontrolled ( )

TABLE OF CONTENTS

ISSUE HISTORY

ISSUE NO.	DATE	DESCRIPTION	REVISED BY	APPROVED BY
A	10 August 1993	Issued		

1.0 PURPOSE

The purpose of this procedure is to maintain a system for ensuring that products which are nonconforming are promptly identified, segregated, documented, and dispositioned in accordance with company policy and customer requirements.

2.0 SCOPE

This quality system procedure applies to all nonconformities detected in contract-related products and that cannot be immediately rectified.

3.0 DEFINITIONS

3.1 Nonconformance

A deficiency in characteristics, documentation, or process implementation which renders the quality of an item indeterminate or outside that required by the relevant specification, contract or regulation.

4.0 REFERENCE MATERIAL

QP.09B – In-process and Final Inspection and Testing
QP.12 – Corrective Action

5.0 RESPONSIBILITIES

5.1 Quality Manager

The quality manager is responsible for:

(a) monitoring the adequacy of disposition and the need for corrective action associated with nonconformities;
(b) the control of nonconformance reports and other associated documents.

5.2 Production Manager

The production manager shall be responsible for the evaluation and timely and effective disposition of the nonconforming work.

5.3 QC Inspector

The QC inspector shall be responsible for identifying, recording and isolating nonconforming products and the re-inspection of repaired and/or reworked products.

6.0 PROCEDURE

Upon completion of inspection activities in accordance with procedure (QP.09B), or in any other instances (e.g. general surveillance inspection), nonconforming work shall be isolated for disposition wherever possible by the QC inspector, in consultation with the production manager.

6.1 Holding Area

The intended purpose of a holding area is to facilitate isolation of nonconforming work from the workplace, pending disposition. The production manager shall ensure that a holding area is provided in or adjacent to the work area. The holding area shall be adequately sized and equipped with shelving suitable for the short-term storage of nonconforming product.

The holding area shall not be used for other than its intended purpose. The production manager shall ensure that his supervisory staff and QC inspectors adhere to and enforce this requirement.

6.2 Isolation of Nonconforming Products

QC inspectors shall identify nonconforming products and bring them to the attention of the quality manager and production manager by way of a nonconformance report form. The QC inspector shall cause the product to be immediately removed from the location where the nonconformance was discovered and placed in the holding area pending disposition.

The production manager shall evaluate the nonconformance to determine the seriousness of the deficiency on impact on production and delivery.

If it is impractical to deal with large or heavy nonconforming work in this manner, the QC inspector shall arrange for the work to be clearly labelled as nonconforming.

6.3 Nonconformance Reports

The QC inspector shall issue the nonconformance report to the production manager and quality manager.

6.3.1 Content

The nonconformance report should identify the following, as applicable:

(a) Nonconformance report number
(b) Job number
(c) Customer order number
(d) Description of the nonconformance
(e) Proposed disposition and resulting rectification, reinspection or retesting

Details of the nonconformance report including number, date registered, disposition and close out date shall be recorded in a register held in the quality manager's office (a suitable book). The nonconformance report number shall take the form of NCR no.: /01, where:

(a) the "NCR no." is a permanent feature of the report number;
(b) 01 is the first number and continues with 02, 03, 04, etc.

6.3.2 Distribution

Nonconformance reports shall be distributed as follows:

- Original – production manager
- Copies – quality manager

6.4 Disposition

Disposition of nonconforming products may be as follows:

(a) Scrap
(b) Rework or repair
(c) Use-as-is (written customer concession must be obtained)
(d) Downgrade (use for other purpose)

The method of disposition of the nonconforming product shall be decided by the production manager, after consultation with any appropriate personnel. This shall be documented in the nonconformance report and the applicable nonconforming product shall be marked accordingly.

Where it is decided and agreed that a concession will be applied to accept the nonconformance "as is", then application shall be made in writing to the customer. Any concession shall in turn be obtained in writing and shall be filed with the job file as a quality record (see QP.14).

Where a contract requires repairs to be acknowledged to the customer, this shall also be in writing and all communications/approvals shall be retained as quality records.

6.5 Close-out of the Nonconformance

The quality manager shall monitor the progress and resolution of nonconformances. If unsuitable action has not been taken within an appropriate time, the quality manager shall refer the matter to the managing director.

The QC inspector shall sign off the nonconformance report to close out the nonconformance subsequent to a direct review of the item concerned and/or a review of the documented objective evidence where appropriate.

6.6 Recurring Nonconformances

The quality manager shall maintain a file of nonconformance reports and produce findings in sufficient detail to indicate recurring nonconformances which require corrective action (see QP.12).

APPENDIX

1. Nonconformance Report (QP.11.01)

APPENDIX 1

NONCONFORMANCE REPORT

Job no.: Customer ref. no.: NCR no.:

Project:

Purchase order no.:

Description of nonconformance:

Prepared by: Date:

Proposed disposition action:

1. Rework to meet specification ☐ 2. Scrap ☐

3. Repair ☐ 4. Use-as-is* ☐

Prepared by: Date:

Proposed action approval: Approved ☐ Not approved** ☐

* Concession request ref.: ______________________________

** Comments: ______________________________

Signed: Date:

Verification of any rectification or rework:

____

____

____

____

Signed: Date:

QP.11.01 Version 1

ABC COMPANY

QUALITY SYSTEM PROCEDURE

FOR

CORRECTIVE ACTION

DOCUMENT NO.: QP.12

	NAME	SIGNATURE	DATE
PREPARED BY:			
APPROVED BY:			

Copy no.: ______________

Controlled ( )

Uncontrolled ( )

TABLE OF CONTENTS

ISSUE HISTORY

ISSUE NO.	DATE	DESCRIPTION	REVISED BY	APPROVED BY
A	10 August 1993	Issued		

1.0 PURPOSE

The purpose of this procedure is to maintain a system for controlling conditions within the company which are adverse to quality by finding the root cause of the problem, correcting the cause and taking action to prevent a recurrence of the problem.

2.0 SCOPE

This procedure applies to:

(a) actions necessary to resolve noncompliances found during auditing of the quality system;
(b) actions necessary to resolve nonconforming product;
(c) customer complaints;
(d) problems identified by management.

3.0 DEFINITIONS

3.1 Nonconformance

A deficiency in characteristics, documentation or process implementation which renders the quality of a product indeterminate or outside that required by the relevant specification, contract or regulation.

3.2 Noncompliance

A deficiency in the quality system whereby personnel are not following specified, documented planned arrangements and/or procedures.

4.0 REFERENCE MATERIAL

QP.02 – Management Review
QP.11 – Control of Nonconforming Product
QP.15 – Internal Quality Audits

5.0 RESPONSIBILITIES

5.1 Quality Manager

The quality manager is responsible for:

(a) raising corrective action requests as a result of serious or repetitive nonconformances, customer complaints and as directed by management during management review (see QP.02);
(b) receiving, evaluating and recording customer complaints;
(c) maintaining the corrective action request status log;
(d) monitoring the status log to ensure corrective actions are closed out.

5.2 Auditor

The auditor is responsible for:

(a) raising a corrective action request as a result of internal quality audits;
(b) conducting the follow-up audit.

5.3 Production Manager

The production manager is responsible for:

(a) the timely initiation of action to identify the root cause of a nonconformance or noncompliance;
(b) proposing all corrective actions;
(c) initiating effective and timely preventive action.

6.0 PROCEDURE

Corrective action requests may be raised as a result of the following:

(a) Noncompliances detected during scheduled and unscheduled audits (*Note:* Unscheduled audits may be directed at management review.)
(b) Serious nonconformances
(c) Recurring nonconformances (see QP.11)
(d) Customer complaints
(e) Management review

6.1 Quality System Noncompliances

When noncompliances in the quality system are identified through either scheduled or unscheduled audits (see QP.15), they shall be documented on a corrective action request.

The auditor shall prepare and issue the corrective action requests, verify that corrective action has occurred, and summarise the records on the corrective action status log.

If the noncompliance is deemed justified by the auditor, it shall be reflected in a revision to the procedures, otherwise corrective action shall be taken without undue delay. The auditor or quality manager shall maintain follow-up audits until the noncompliance is rectified.

6.2 Quality of Products

The quality manager shall maintain a file of nonconformance reports and record findings in sufficient detail to indicate recurring nonconformances which require corrective action.

Serious or repetitive nonconformances in products (see QP.11) shall be documented on a corrective action request raised by the quality manager.

The corrective action request shall be completed and returned to the quality manager by the production manager.

The quality manager shall determine whether the recommended corrective action is satisfactory, and, shall verify that the corrective action has been effectively implemented.

The quality manager shall maintain a record file of documented corrective actions.

In cases where the corrective action cannot be satisfactorily resolved by the quality manager, it shall be referred to the managing director for resolution.

6.3 Customer Complaints

Customer complaints shall be directed to the quality manager who maintains a complaints register.

When a customer reports that a practice being followed by ABC Company is producing unsatisfactory results or a lack of control, the quality manager shall be requested to initiate action to review the practice against the approved procedure and issue a corrective action request, as appropriate, to be processed in the normal manner.

In all cases of customer complaints, the quality manager shall report to the managing director the nature, status and action of the complaint.

There shall be confirmation of the resolution of all actions in this category of complaint.

6.4 Management Review

During management review (see QP.02) senior personnel may identify problems relating to the quality of products or in the quality management system. If a problem is clearly identified, management shall direct the quality manager to initiate a corrective action request.

6.5 Corrective Action Requests (CAR)

6.5.1 Raising the CAR

6.5.1.1 CAR number If the quality manager or auditor decides to issue a corrective action request he shall commence by raising a CAR number. The CAR number shall take the following form:

Audit-related CARs
Audit Report No. /01

where:

(a) the "Audit Report No." is the number of the associated audit report (see QP.15);
(b) 01 is the number of the first deficiency found and numbering continues with 02, 03, 04, etc.

Complaints, Nonconformances and Management Review

In the case of CARs raised as a result of repetitive or serious nonconformances, customer complaints and/or management review, the CAR number assigned shall be CAR/01 where:

(a) "CAR" is a fixed word to indicate that the CAR was not raised through the audit process;
(b) "01" is a continuation of the system demonstrated above.

6.5.1.2 Content When raising a CAR, the quality manager or auditor shall ensure completion of the form (see Appendix 1) as follows:

(a) Department – state the name and address of the auditee department.
(b) Audit criteria – state the title of the procedure or document relating to the problem.
(c) Auditor – state the name of the person who identified the problem.
(d) Department representative – the name of the person to whom the CAR was issued.
(e) Deficiency – state the details of the noncompliance, nonconformance or complaint.

6.5.1.3 Deficiency – signatures Having completed the CAR to this stage, the quality manager shall obtain the signature of the representative of department where the problem has been identified acknowledging the deficiency.

It is important to emphasise that the signature from the company/department representative only indicates his understanding of the problem addressed and not necessarily agreement.

The quality manager/auditor shall then sign the CAR.

6.5.1.4 Distribution Having signed the CAR, the quality manager/auditor shall provide copies to the manager of the area where the problem is identified.

In the case of an audit, the original CAR shall be retained for formal issue to the auditee with a copy of the audit report (see QP.15).

Copies of the CAR and, where applicable, the audit report shall be forwarded to the quality manager.

6.5.2 CAR Status Log

The quality manager shall update the corrective action request status log (see Appendix 2).

6.5.3 Action by the Department Representative

The department representative shall complete the relevant sections of the CAR as follows:

(a) Corrective action – state the action to be taken to correct the deficiency and the date by which it will be implemented. The department representative shall then sign and date the form.
(b) Action taken to prevent recurrence – state the action taken to prevent a recurrence of the deficiency and the date by which this action shall be implemented. Sign and date the statements made.

When the original of the CAR has been completed and returned by the department representatives, the quality manager/auditor shall:

(a) complete the "Proposed Follow-up Date" on the CAR;
(b) complete the "Proposed Follow-up Date" on the CAR status log.

6.5.4 Close Out

A follow-up shall be undertaken to verify the implementation of the action taken to correct the deficiency.

If the action taken is satisfactory, the quality manager/auditor shall complete the "Follow-up and Close Out" section of the CAR referencing the verification and, signing and dating the CAR as being "Closed Out".

The auditor, and/or quality manager, shall complete the relevant sections of the CAR status log.

6.5.5 Re-addressing a Deficiency

When a follow-up indicates that the actions taken have not been effective in correcting the deficiency and/or preventing recurrence, this shall be recorded and this CAR shall be closed out.

The continuing deficiency shall be re-addressed by a new CAR. The number of the new CAR shall be cross referenced to the old CAR and vice versa.

Should the follow-up indicate that the action taken is still unsatisfactory, the CAR shall be forwarded to the managing director for further action.

6.5.6 Monitoring the CAR Status Log

The quality manager shall review the CAR status log on a regular basis and should a response to any CAR be overdue, a reminder shall be sent to the department representative requesting a response.

If no response is received within one week of the reminder date, the subject shall be passed to the managing director for further action.

6.6 Records

The quality manager shall maintain files of all documents which contain data associated with noncompliances.

APPENDIXES

1. Corrective Action Request (QP.12.01)
2. Corrective Action Request (CAR) Status Log (QP.12.02)

APPENDIX 1

CORRECTIVE ACTION REQUEST		
Audit [ ] No.: ______ Complaint [ ] NCR [ ]	CAR no.: ________	Date: __________
Department:		
Audit criteria:		
Auditor:	Department representative:	
Deficiency: Signature: ____________________ Signature: ____________________ Department representative Auditor/Quality manager		
Corrective action Date for completion of corrective action: ____________________ Signature: ____________________ Date: ____________________ Department representative		
Action taken to prevent recurrence of problem Date for completion of action to prevent recurrence: ____________________ Signature: ____________________ Date: ____________________ Department representative		
Follow-up and close out Proposed follow-up date: ____________________ Follow-up details CAR close out date: ____________ Signature: ____________________		

QP.12.01 Version 1

APPENDIX 2

CORRECTIVE ACTION REQUEST (CAR) STATUS LOG

CAR no.	CAR issued to	Date CAR issued	Response due date to CAR	Corrective action completion date	Recurrence action completion date	Proposed follow-up date	Date CAR closed

QP.12.02 Version 1

ABC COMPANY

QUALITY SYSTEM PROCEDURE

FOR

HANDLING, STORAGE, PACKAGING AND DELIVERY

DOCUMENT NO.: QP.13

	NAME	SIGNATURE	DATE
PREPARED BY:			
APPROVED BY:			

Copy no.: ____________

Controlled ( )

Uncontrolled ( )

TABLE OF CONTENTS

ISSUE HISTORY

ISSUE NO.	DATE	DESCRIPTION	REVISED BY	APPROVED BY
A	23 August 1993	Issued		

1.0 PURPOSE

The purpose of this quality system procedure is to provide a system for the handling and storage of goods prior to and during manufacture. The procedure further defines a system for packaging and ensuring the timely delivery of goods.

2.0 SCOPE

This quality system procedure applies to all materials, products and consumables handled by ABC Company Pty Ltd.

3.0 DEFINITIONS

Nil

4.0 REFERENCE MATERIAL

QP.07 – Product Identification and Traceability

5.0 RESPONSIBILITIES

5.1 Production Manager

The production manager shall:

- ensure that general storage areas are provided and maintained where applicable;
- provide work procedures to the storeman, detailing special contract requirements for the handling, storage, packaging and delivery of goods for specific contract works.

5.2 Storeman

The storeman shall ensure the handling, storage, packaging and delivery requirements defined in this procedure are adhered to at all times.

6.0 PROCEDURE

6.1 General

The system for identification of materials and equipment at all stages of manufacture is detailed in procedure QP.07.

The production manager is responsible for monitoring the handling, storage, packaging and delivery of all materials. He shall ensure that company policy, statutory and order requirements are always adhered to. For non-standard or special order requirements, the production manager shall communicate such requirements using written work procedures.

6.2 Handling

6.2.1 Most items handled by ABC Company do not generally require special attention, however, where it is an order requirement, the production manager shall advise the storeman (and all other relevant staff) accordingly of any handling requirements.

6.2.2 The production manager shall be responsible for ensuring all items are handled in such a manner as to protect against abuse, damage, deterioration or contamination.

6.3 Storage

6.3.1 The production manager shall ensure that stores are provided and maintained where applicable. These storage areas shall facilitate proper control of goods and provide protection against harmful environmental factors. To this end, the storeman shall ensure the nominated areas are adequately bordered, secured and sheltered.

6.3.2 All purchased goods shall be stored in identifiable and secure locations. The production manager shall periodically inspect storage conditions and verify shelf life of chemicals.

6.3.3 Welding consumables shall be stored at the temperatures and environmental conditions specified by the manufacturer.

This may involve baking prior to issue to the workshop operators. After issue, low hydrogen electrodes shall be held in quivers at the temperatures nominated in welding procedures.

6.3.4 Goods arriving into stores shall be listed onto a ledger which shall be maintained to identify the current stock levels and the date of issue of contract-related items.

6.4 Packaging and Packing

In general, no special packaging or preservation requirements are required for orders undertaken by ABC Company. However, where it is an order requirement, the production manager shall advise the storeman of any special packaging and preservation requirements.

All goods shall be identified and marked prior to packaging, as required by the customer, or established practice.

6.5 Delivery

6.5.1 The storeman shall ensure that all items are delivered in a manner to prevent loss, damage, or deterioration and ensure timely arrival.

6.5.2 Prior to despatch, the storeman shall verify packages to ensure:

(a) the address and markings are correct on the package and all associated freight documentation describing packages contents is included;
(b) all relevant certification has been included with the package.

The production manager shall advise the storeman of any special delivery requirements specified by the customer.

ABC COMPANY

QUALITY SYSTEM PROCEDURE

FOR

QUALITY RECORDS

DOCUMENT NO.: QP.14

	NAME	SIGNATURE	DATE
PREPARED BY:			
APPROVED BY:			

Copy no.: ______________

Controlled ( )

Uncontrolled ( )

TABLE OF CONTENTS

ISSUE HISTORY

ISSUE NO.	DATE	DESCRIPTION	REVISED BY	APPROVED BY
A	23 August 1993	Issued		

1.0 PURPOSE

The objective of this quality system procedure is to establish and maintain a system for retaining records which provide objective evidence that:

(a) the company quality system meets the requirements stated in the quality policy manual and referenced procedures;
(b) the company's products meet the requirements of a customer order.

2.0 SCOPE

This quality system procedure applies to all records (hard copy or electronic media) generated by the quality system as defined in the various procedures.

3.0 DEFINITIONS

Nil

4.0 REFERENCE MATERIAL

Nil

5.0 RESPONSIBILITIES

5.1 Employees

Employees who generate records are responsible for identifying, collating, filing, indexing and maintaining those records as specified in the quality policy manual, quality system procedures or work procedures.

5.2 Quality Manager

The quality manager is responsible for:

(a) retaining all quality system related records for a period of three years, except training records which shall be retained for the period of time the person remains in employment and calibration records for the life of the equipment;
(b) disposing of quality system records after the storage period has expired.

5.3 Production Manager

The production manager is responsible for:

(a) retaining all job related records for one year after expiry of contract warranty;
(b) disposing of job related records after the storage period has expired.

5.4 Document Controller

The document controller is responsible for the archival storage of all records as defined by the production or quality manager.

6.0 PROCEDURE

6.1 General

Records generated and maintained by the company constitute the objective evidence necessary to demonstrate:

(a) the conformance of the company quality system to the requirements stated in the quality policy manual and referenced procedures;
(b) the conformance of the company's products to the requirements of customer orders or contracts.

Quality records are generated by many personnel throughout ABC Company and must be identified, filed and maintained in such a manner that makes them readily identifiable and retrievable when necessary.

6.2 Quality System Records

Quality system records include, but are not limited to, the following:

(a) Audit reports
(b) Corrective action requests
(c) Statistical records
(d) Training and certification records
(e) Supplier assessment records
(f) Equipment calibration and maintenance records
(g) Management review meeting minutes

Each of these constitutes part of the objective evidence required to verify the operation, status and maintenance of the company's quality system.

The responsibility for generating and maintaining these records is identified in the appropriate section of the quality policy manual or quality system procedures.

Personnel responsible for generating and maintaining these records shall do so in accordance with instructions laid down in relevant procedures.

6.3 Records Associated with a Contract

Records associated with a contract include, but are not limited to, the following:

(a) Customer specifications and drawings
(b) ABC Company's generated specification and drawings
(c) Test certificates
(d) Inspection and test records
(e) Subcontractor supplied records
(f) Contract review records
(g) Nonconformance reports
(h) Purchaser-supplied product records

Each of these constitutes part of the objective evidence necessary to verify conformance to the requirements of the company's work. The responsibility for generating and maintaining these records is identified under the appropriate quality system procedure or work procedure. Personnel responsible for generating and maintaining these records shall do so in accordance with instructions laid down in relevant procedures.

6.4 Retention of Records

Quality system records shall be maintained by the quality manager. They shall be identified, filed and stored in a historical sequence to provide ready and easy access for the company and customer's representatives.

Contract-related records shall be maintained under the direction of the production manager. They shall be identified under the appropriate job number, filed, and stored on a job-by-job basis.

6.5 Archival Storage

All records shall be maintained in an environment that protects them from deterioration or damage.

The document controller shall ensure that all records are retained for a minimum period of three years unless otherwise specified by order or legislative requirements. The decision to dispose of records at any stage shall be made after consultation with the managing director.

The document controller shall maintain an archiving register and index system so that all archived records remain traceable for the duration of storage.

APPENDIX

1. Quality Records Index (QP.14.01)

APPENDIX 1

QUALITY RECORDS INDEX Page of

DESCRIPTION	LOCATION	FILE IDENTIFICATION SYSTEM	RETENTION PERIOD

QP.14.01 Version 1

ABC COMPANY

QUALITY SYSTEM PROCEDURE

FOR

INTERNAL QUALITY AUDITS

DOCUMENT NO.: QP.15

	NAME	SIGNATURE	DATE
PREPARED BY:			
APPROVED BY:			

Copy no.: ____________

Controlled ( )

Uncontrolled ( )

TABLE OF CONTENTS

ISSUE HISTORY

ISSUE NO.	DATE	DESCRIPTION	REVISED BY	APPROVED BY
A	23 August 1993	Issued		

1.0 PURPOSE

The purpose of this procedure is to establish the criteria, methods and responsibilities for the execution of internal quality audits to verify the implementation and effectiveness of the quality management system. Verification shall be by means of a uniform and controlled method for planning, scheduling, co-ordinating and performing audits, and assigning responsibilities for these activities.

2.0 SCOPE

This procedure applies to all internal quality audits performed by nominated ABC Company's personnel.

3.0 DEFINITIONS

Nil

4.0 REFERENCE MATERIAL

QP.02 – Management Review
QP.12 – Corrective Action
QP.14 – Quality Records

5.0 RESPONSIBILITIES

5.1 Quality Manager

The quality manager is responsible for:

- establishing and maintaining audit schedules;
- planning, co-ordinating, and analysing the results of the quality audits;
- reviewing the audit report;
- initiating unscheduled audits.

5.2 Auditor

The nominated auditor shall be responsible for planning, performing, and reporting the audit.

5.3 Auditee

It is the responsibility of the auditee to review the deficiencies noted during the audit and take the necessary corrective action.

6.0 PROCEDURE

6.1 Audit Scheduling

6.1.1 The quality manager shall establish and approve an audit schedule (see Appendix 1) to ensure that all aspects of the quality system are subjected to audit on a regular basis (e.g. every six months).

Unscheduled audits may be added to the schedule when a serious breakdown in the quality system is detected or as a result of management review.

6.1.2 The audit schedule shall be reviewed by the quality manager on a regular basis and updated as necessary. The date of each audit shall be recorded on the audit schedule. Where undesirable trends are evident, the audit schedule may be revised to arrange for an audit of the applicable areas involved.

6.2 Preparation and Planning of Audits

6.2.1 The quality manager shall be responsible for planning and nominating auditors, who will conduct and report the audit in accordance with the requirements of this procedure.

6.2.2 The auditor shall number the audit with the next available number from the audit register (see Appendix 2) and enter other details as far as possible.

6.2.3 The auditor shall advise the auditee in advance of the intent to audit.

6.3 Performance of the Audit

6.3.1 Audits should normally commence with an introductory meeting attended by all key personnel. The following will be outlined:

- Scope and schedule for the audit
- Method of recording noncompliances
- Close out meeting arrangements

6.3.2 The auditor shall seek evidence of compliance with the requirements of procedures, instructions, methods, etc. Such evidence shall be sought against a prepared checklist taken from company procedures and other documented requirements.

Compliance checks shall be sought by sampling records and observation of activity. The results of the sampling and observation shall be recorded on the audit checklist.

6.3.3 The auditor shall classify audit findings as follows:

- Corrective Action (C) – where there is a breakdown in the system caused by non-adherence to procedures and planned arrangements.
- Acceptable (A) – no deficiencies detected.
- Observation (O) – where the basic intent has been met but the procedure or practice could be improved to provide better assurance of compliance.

6.4 Corrective Action Request (CAR)

When completing a CAR, the auditor shall complete the form as detailed in procedure QP.12.

6.5 Close Out of Audit

6.5.1 At the close out meeting, the auditor shall present an objective overview of the audit results. Noncomplying aspects of the audit shall be presented in the form of CARs.

6.5.2 The CAR shall be completed as far as practical during the meeting, copied for information of the audited department and the original retained by the quality manager for follow-up.

6.6 Audit Report

A formal audit report to management shall be prepared by the auditor. The audit checklist and any CAR shall be listed and/or attached. Distribution of the audit report shall be as determined by the quality manager but will always be presented at management review (QP.02).

6.7 Follow-up Audit

6.7.1 The quality manager shall enter the CAR detail on the status log and follow-up by the due date.

6.7.2 When the follow-up audit indicates that the nominated actions taken have been implemented and are effective, the quality manager shall close out the CAR as defined in QP.12.

6.7.3 A copy of the closed out CAR is distributed to recipients of the initial audit report and the status log updated.

6.7.4 The quality manager shall retain and file all audit reports, attachments, CARs and the results of audits as quality records in accordance with procedure QP.14.

APPENDIXES

1. Audit Schedule (QP.15.01)
2. Audit Register (QP.15.02)
3. Audit Checklist (QP.15.03)
4. Audit Report Lead Sheet (QP.15.04)
5. Audit Report Sheet (QP.15.05)

APPENDIX 1

AUDIT SCHEDULE	Prepared by:									Date:		
	Approved by:									Date:		
ACTIVITY TO BE AUDITED	Rev. no.:						Year:					
	JAN	FEB	MAR	APR	MAY	JUN	JUL	AUG	SEP	OCT	NOV	DEC

Date schedule reviewed				

QP.15.01 Version 1

APPENDIX 2

AUDIT REGISTER						
Audit number	Audit date	Department or area audited	Scope/ Procedure	Nominated auditor	No. of CARs issued	Follow-up (if applicable)

QP.15.02 Version 1

APPENDIX 3

AUDIT CHECKLIST			
Audit no.:		Page ____ of ____	
Question no.	Question	Category (A/O/C)	Remarks

QP.15.03 Version 1

APPENDIX 4

AUDIT REPORT LEAD SHEET		
Audited department/organisation:		
Audit date:	Audit no.:	
Auditees:	No. of CARs:	No. of observations:
Audit team:	Reference documents:	
Summary:		
Prepared by: Date:	Approved by: Date:	Distribution:

QP.15.04 Version 1

APPENDIX 5

AUDIT REPORT SHEET	
Audit no.:	Page of

QP.15.05 Version 1

ABC COMPANY

QUALITY SYSTEM PROCEDURE

FOR

TRAINING

DOCUMENT NO.: QP.16

	NAME	SIGNATURE	DATE
PREPARED BY:			
APPROVED BY:			

Copy no.: ____________

Controlled ( )

Uncontrolled ( )

TABLE OF CONTENTS

ISSUE HISTORY

ISSUE NO.	DATE	DESCRIPTION	REVISED BY	APPROVED BY
A	23 August 1993	Issued		

1.0 PURPOSE

This quality system procedure defines a system for identifying, implementing and recording staff training programmes within ABC Company.

2.0 SCOPE

This procedure applies to all staff of ABC Company.

3.0 DEFINITIONS

Nil

4.0 REFERENCE MATERIAL

QP.02 – Management Review
QP.03 – Contract Review
QP.14 – Quality Records

5.0 RESPONSIBILITIES

5.1 Managing Director

The managing director shall:

- identify training requirements during contract review and management review meetings;
- support training initiatives prepared by senior personnel.

5.2 Production Manager

The production manager shall have overall responsibility for identifying and initiating training programmes.

5.3 Quality Manager

The quality manager shall identify and implement training programmes related to the quality system.

6.0 PROCEDURE

6.1 General

The nature of the company's activities are such that the majority of technical activities are undertaken by qualified and experienced personnel within their discipline. However, a system shall be maintained to identify additional training needs and certification requirements, and to provide records of such training programmes.

6.2 Establishing Requirements

The requirement for additional training shall be identified by the managing director during contract reviews (see QP.03) and management review meetings (see QP.02). The production manager and other senior personnel may identify additional training requirements during their normal activities. The production manager shall initiate training in accordance with the provisions defined in this procedure.

Training requirements may be identified from the following:

- Change in job description
- Induction of new personnel
- Introduction of new technology
- Corporate strategic planning
- Quality audit findings

6.3 Training Categories

Two types of training requirements are recognised as set out in the following paragraphs.

6.3.1 On-the-job Training

This training is provided by company personnel who are competent in the subject task and are considered by the production manager as being able to impart such skills to another person.

6.3.2 Formal Training

This training is provided when on-the-job training is considered inappropriate or inadequate by the production manager. Where the need for formal training is identified, the production manager shall appoint a suitably qualified individual or organisation to prepare and conduct the training programme.

6.4 Quality System Training

All personnel shall be trained in the use and philosophies of ABC Company's quality management system. The quality manager shall co-ordinate and instigate induction sessions for new employees who will be made familiar with the requirements of the quality policy manual, policies and quality system procedures.

The quality manager shall ensure that all internal auditors are trained and assessed in their knowledge of quality system standards and appropriate audit techniques, prior to conducting an audit.

6.5 Training Records

Personnel files for all company employees shall be opened and maintained. The managing director, or his nominee, shall establish records of all training received by personnel, using the employee training record (see Appendix 1). Training records shall be retained as defined in procedure QP.14.

Work skills shall be assessed and recorded, as appropriate, during the initial job interview. Copies of trade, professional and other qualification documents shall be filed on the employee's training file.

At periodic intervals, the production manager shall review all training files to monitor status of expirable certification and permits to arrange timely re-endorsement training.

APPENDIX

1. Employee Training Record (QP.16.01)

APPENDIX 1

EMPLOYEE TRAINING RECORD

Full name:	Date of birth:	Payroll no.:
Position:	Education/Qualifications:	
Membership of professional bodies:		

ATTENDANCE AT COURSES, SEMINARS, etc.

DATE	DURATION	NAME/TITLE/REFERENCE OF COURSE	COURSE DESCRIPTION/DETAILS	PRESENTER/INSTITUTION

QP.16.01 Version 1

ABC COMPANY

QUALITY SYSTEM PROCEDURE

FOR

STATISTICAL PROCESS MONITORING

DOCUMENT NO.: QP.17

	NAME	SIGNATURE	DATE
PREPARED BY:			
APPROVED BY:			

Copy no.: ____________

Controlled ( )

Uncontrolled ( )

TABLE OF CONTENTS

ISSUE HISTORY

ISSUE NO.	DATE	DESCRIPTION	REVISED BY	APPROVED BY
A	23 December 1993	Issued		

1.0 PURPOSE

The objective of this quality system procedure is to define a system for monitoring the adequacy of the manufacturing process used within the ABC Company.

2.0 SCOPE

This procedure applies to all manufacturing processes engaged within ABC Company.

3.0 DEFINITIONS

Nil

4.0 REFERENCE MATERIAL

QP.02 – Management Review
QP.11 – Control of Nonconforming Product
QP.12 – Corrective Action

5.0 RESPONSIBILITIES

5.1 Quality Manager

The quality manager is responsible for reviewing all nonconformance reports raised and plotting statistics in a graphical manner to review the adequacy of process controls and product characteristics.

6.0 PROCEDURE

6.1 The quality manager receives copies of all nonconformance reports (NCRs) raised within the company. At the end of each calendar month, the quality manager totals up:

(a) the total number of NCRs raised, and
(b) the total manhours recorded on each NCR that have been expended in the handling, review and dispositioning of each nonconformance.

6.2 The total number of NCRs raised is divided by the total number of units produced for the month and multiplied by 100, to give the "nonconforming product ratio". This ratio is plotted against time as shown in Appendix 1.

That is, $$\text{Nonconforming product ratio} = \frac{\text{No. of NCRs}}{\text{No. of units produced}} \times 100$$

6.3 The total number of manhours expended on each nonconformance is divided by the total manhours worked by the production department and multiplied by 100. This ratio is plotted against time as shown in Appendix 2. This is known as the "cost of nonconformance ratio".

That is, $$\text{Cost of nonconformance ratio} = \frac{\text{NCR manhours}}{\text{Total production manhours}} \times 100$$

6.4 These process ratios are plotted on an annual basis with occasional sporadic shifts on the plot monitored by the quality manager for any *trends* upwards or downwards. Reactions to occasional sporadic spikes should be avoided unless an obvious root cause is quickly determined. In any cases where trends show a deterioration in process control, corrective action shall be implemented as defined in QP.12.

6.5 Overall trends are reviewed at management meetings (QP.02) whereby process improvements and future targets for statistical ratios are agreed upon.

APPENDIXES

1. Nonconforming Product Ratio Chart (QP.17.01)
2. Cost of Nonconformance Ratio Chart (QP.17.02)

APPENDIX 1

NONCONFORMING PRODUCT RATIO

YEAR: ____________

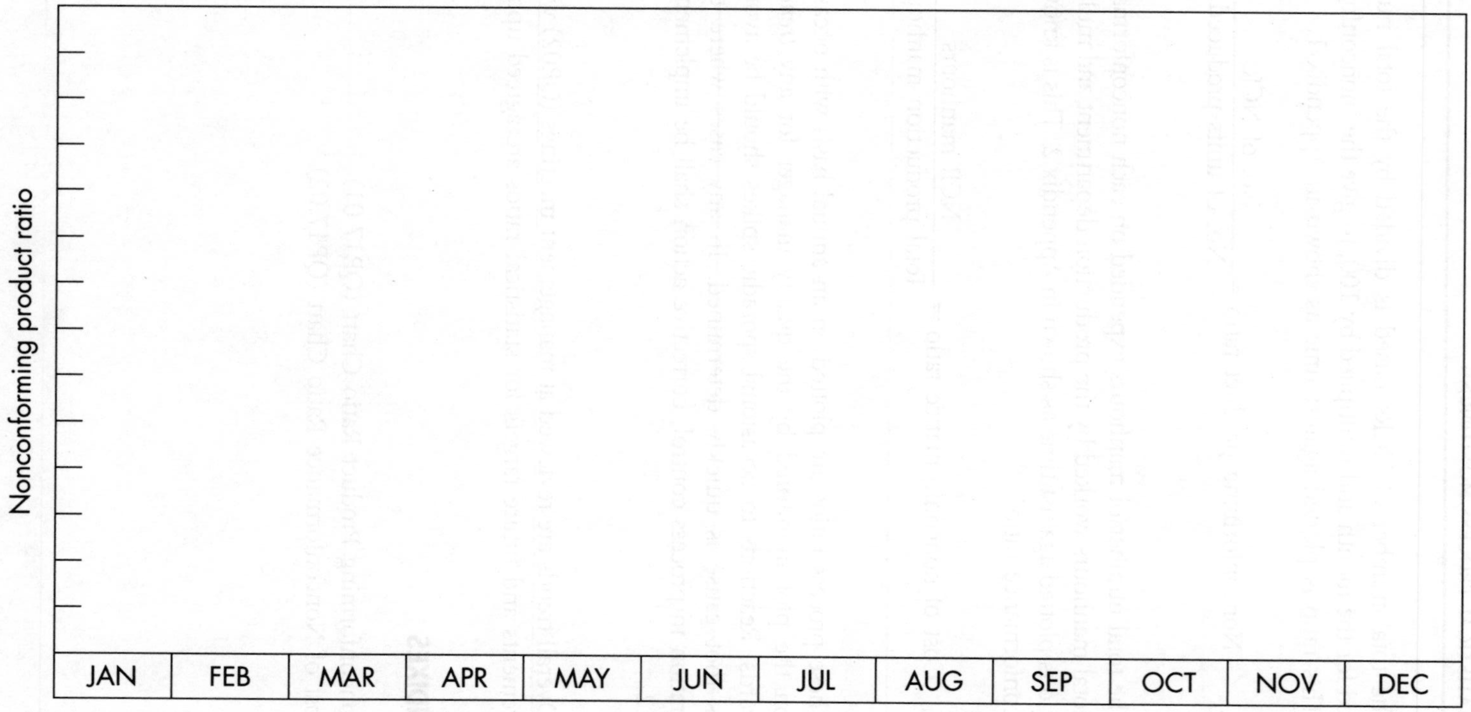
Nonconforming product ratio
JAN
FEB
MAR
APR
MAY
JUN
JUL
AUG
SEP
OCT
NOV
DEC

QP.17.01 Version 1

APPENDIX 2

COST OF NONCONFORMANCE RATIO

YEAR: ____________________

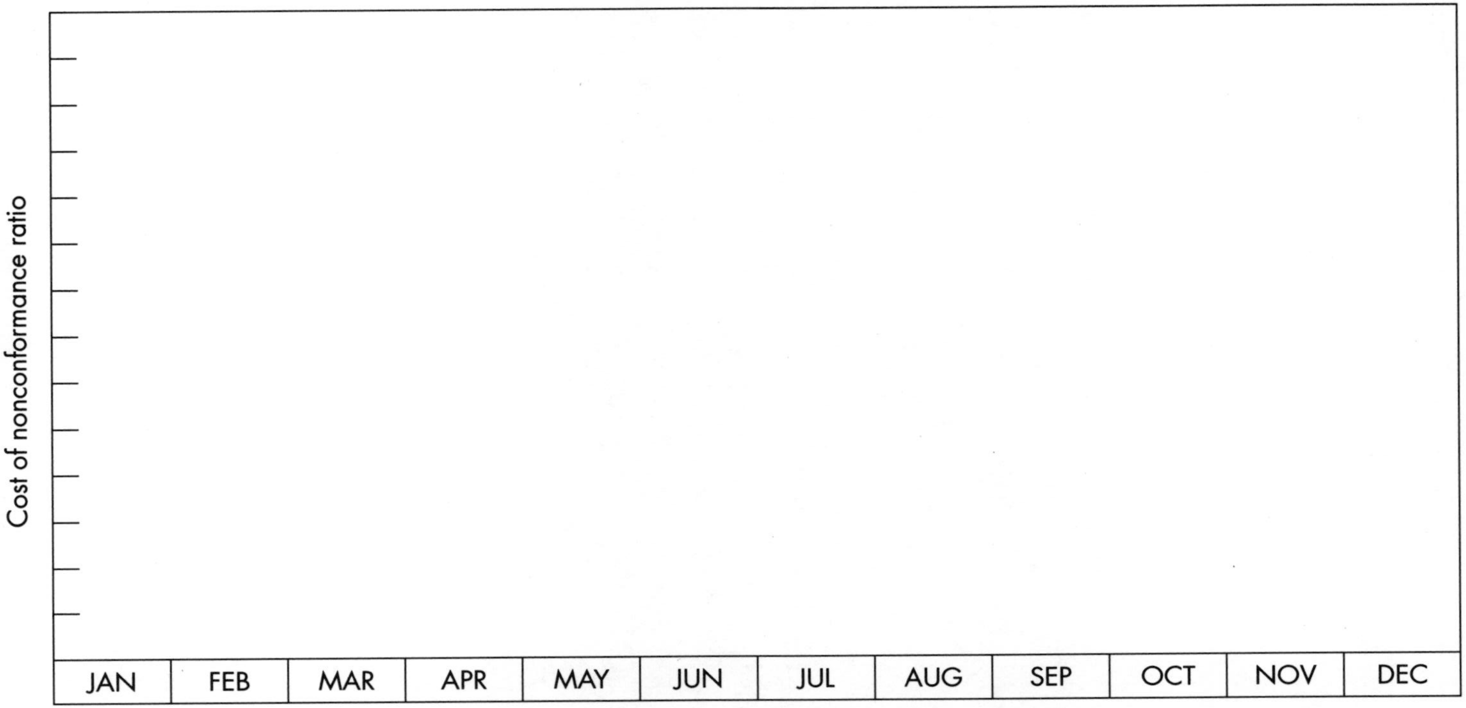
Cost of nonconformance ratio
JAN
FEB
MAR
APR
MAY
JUN
JUL
AUG
SEP
OCT
NOV
DEC

QP.17.02 Version 1

STEP 6

AUDITING

6.1 PLANNING

The definition of a quality audit is:

> a systematic and independent examination to determine whether quality activities and related results comply with planned arrangements and whether these arrangements are implemented effectively and are suitable to achieve objectives (ISO 8402).

Internal audits, system reviews, management reviews, etc., should all be viewed as ongoing activities, continually assessing the effectiveness of the quality system and recommending corrective actions to maintain the required standards. They should be carried out by personnel who are independent of the areas being audited or reviewed.

The benefits of starting internal audits at an early stage are:

- the lessons and experience which can be applied to documentation still being developed (without the need for full-scale revisions at a later date);
- the increased awareness of, and familiarity with, the quality system by all personnel;
- the training and development of auditors' expertise as well as preparing the auditees for the assessment/certification process.

The steps involved in planning an audit are:

- preparation of the audit schedule;
- appointment of audit team;
- notification to the auditee;
- review documentation and develop checklists.

An internal audit schedule should be established in parallel with the development of the quality system so that, as the quality policy manual and associated quality system and work procedures are produced, they are incorporated into the schedule.

The audit schedule should be produced as a formal document with a pre-determined look-ahead period, e.g. six months. An example of an audit schedule is shown on page 229. Audits can be conducted on either a departmental or functional basis, by quality system element or by procedure, as long as each aspect of the quality system is included at least twice a year. The appointment of the audit team will depend on factors such as experience, qualifications, availability, etc. (see 6.3). The audit schedule should be approved and issued to auditees with sufficient advance notice – auditees should be consulted if necessary to agree on convenient dates. The review of the documentation should involve not only the quality policy manual and procedures, etc., but also previous audit reports and corrective action requests.

6.2 AUDITING TECHNIQUES

The audit process involves developing and using checklists of questions and assessing whether or not there is compliance with the required standard. You may come across the following distinction in audit types:

- *System* audit which involves checking and evaluating the documentation only to determine whether there is a formal quality system in place and whether the system is adequate to meet the company's quality objectives.
- *Compliance* audit which involves checking and evaluating activities and work methods against documented procedures and sighting objective evidence, to determine whether the quality system is being implemented and maintained properly.

Procedure QP.15 of Step 5 is a model procedure on how to undertake an audit, including the preparation of a checklist, obtaining objective evidence, raising corrective action requests (CARs) and reporting findings. Procedure QP.12 of Step 5 is a model procedure on dealing with CARs.

6.3 AUDITORS

ISO 9001 and ISO 9002 require internal audits to be undertaken by personnel independent of the function or activity being audited. Clause 4.1.2.2 of ISO 9001 and ISO 9002 also requires such verification personnel to be appropriately trained.

In addition to the ISO 9000 series of standards, there are three standards which are guidelines on auditing:

ISO 10011.1 – Auditing
ISO 10011.2 – Qualification Criteria for Auditors
ISO 10011.3 – Managing Audit Programmes

You may wish to obtain copies of these standards for use by your chosen audit personnel.

Our recommendation is that your quality representative be nominated as the main auditor, as he is generally the person in your organisation with the most knowledge of your quality systems. Other personnel can be trained "on-the-job" or you can use the services of outside experts, particularly if your quality representative is not experienced in auditing techniques. You may have to demonstrate to the assessors that your auditors have the appropriate training and experience. Remember also that you will need an independent person to audit the audit function.

STEP 7

CERTIFICATION

7.1 ARGUMENTS FOR AND AGAINST

The decision as to whether or not you should obtain formal recognition of the standard of your quality system will depend on what your company perceives to be the benefit of such certification. The term "certification" here is used in the context of an assessment of the quality system by an authorised, independent body, resulting in the award of a certificate if the system is assessed as meeting the requirements of the chosen standard, e.g. ISO 9002. The benefits are usually perceived as:

- demonstrating to clients that a quality system of the required standard is being implemented, i.e. where this may be a pre-requisite in tendering, etc.;
- enhancing the company's competitive position, through use of the assessment body's logo, certificates, etc.;
- increasing or enhancing the morale of the workforce.

The main arguments put forward against certification are:

- the fees of the assessment body, including recurring surveillance audit fees;
- the perception of achieving a "milestone" after which the effort involved in maintaining the quality systems often diminishes.

7.2 ASSESSORS

The better known international organisations which are able to certify quality systems to ISO 9000 are:

- Lloyds Register;
- Bureau Veritas;
- Det Norske Veritas;
- American Bureau of Shipping;
- the national standards organisation in each country which usually operates a separate division for this purpose (e.g. SIRIM in Malaysia, SISIR in Singapore, BSI in United Kingdom and Quality Assurance Services in Australia).

Your choice of assessor may depend on a number of factors such as the type of business you are in, whether or not your clients have any stated preference, and the relative costs and time scales involved.

7.3 CERTIFICATION PROCESS

The process of certification involves the following steps:

- *Application*, to register your intent to seek certification which may involve completion of a standard questionnaire.
- *Pre-assessment visit*, to determine the extent of work required, the time scale and costs and to agree on the scope of the assessment (including the relevant standard).
- *Documentation review*, to assess whether the policies and objectives contained in the quality policy manual are consistent with the requirements of the standard. This review typically takes place up to three months before the actual assessment to allow for any changes in policy and practice to be implemented.
- *Quality system assessment*, which takes place on-site(s) and is carried out in the form of a full-scale compliance audit of all procedures and processes. The full assessment can take up to five days depending on the size of the company.

As in the case of internal audits, the assessors will use the system of issuing nonconformance reports (NCRs) and/or corrective action requests (CARs) to record any deficiencies. These may also be graded according to how serious the deficiency is.

It is normal practice for all major deficiencies to be cleared before award of a certificate, and this may even involve a re-assessment.

Once a certificate has been issued, it is valid for three years but, during that time, the assessors will carry out surveillance audits to ensure that the system is being properly maintained. Such visits are undertaken twice a year.

7.4 COSTS

These will vary between the assessors and will obviously depend on the scope and length of the certification process. On average, the pre-assessment visit may involve 1 day, the documentation review 1–2 days and the final assessment 3–4 days. Surveillance visits will amount to 3–4 days per annum. Most assessors will give an individual quote to every company, depending on the size of the company, scope of assessment and complexity of operations.

ISO 9002-1993/94
THE CHANGES

During the preparation of this handbook the International Standards Committee was in the process of revising the ISO 9002 standard. This chapter provides an explanation of the expected changes with an interpretation of the differences between the 1994 and the 1987 version.

4.1 Management Responsibility

4.1.1 Quality Policy

(i) After "the supplier's management", the words "with executive responsibility for quality" have been included.

This addition has been made as a direction that it is an "executive" or "senior" management responsibility to determine policy. This change is an indication that commitment and drive must come from the top of an organisation and quality policy should be delegated to someone with a specific senior management role.

(ii) A new paragraph has been added stating: "The quality policy shall be relevant to the supplier's organisational goals and the expectations and needs of its customers."

This note reiterates that quality is, and must always be, customer driven. It would be difficult to visualise why a company would define its objectives, goals and policies without taking into consideration its customers' requirements.

The new paragraph is a requirement that the policy as defined in the quality policy manual (quality manual) must reflect truly the supplier's policy and what is necessary to meet the customers' specified requirements.

4.1.2.1 Responsibility and Authority Parts (a) and (b)

A new requirement has been inserted for responsibilities and authorities to be "defined". Whilst "defined" infers that it should be documented, it is not specific. The documenting of responsibilities/authorities is best achieved through job descriptions and the system procedures.

The word "nonconformity" has been removed and the text "process and quality system nonconformities" added to sub-paragraphs (a) and (b).

The 1987 standard only required someone with the authority and responsibility to indicate action to prevent the occurrence of "product" nonconformance. The revised standard has added that the prevention of system deficiencies must also be addressed by a specified function. The identification of action to prevent product deficiencies may be via process control charts and management review; it will often be a production management responsibility. System deficiencies, on the other hand, are usually found through the internal audit system and become a quality manager's responsibility.

4.1.2.2 Verification Resources and Personnel

This clause has been replaced by the following: "The supplier shall identify resource requirements, provide adequate resources and assign trained personnel for management, performance of work and verification activities including internal quality audits."

This clause has omitted the term "in house", allowing the supplier to select from any source its verification resource. This permits, for example, internal audits to be carried out by someone outside the company, maybe a consultant or a reciprocal arrangement with another quality-certified company.

4.1.2.3 Management Representative

The responsibility of the management representative has been expanded and the responsibility for selecting the management representative has been included.

In this respect the wording is now the supplier "management with executive responsibility for quality" shall appoint a member of its own management for review and as a basis for improvement of the quality system.

A new sentence extending the management representative's responsibilities has been added as follows: "The representative has also to report on the performance of the quality system to the supplier's management." The most effective means of meeting this requirement is for the management representative to report quality system performance at the management review meeting.

4.2 Quality System

Three new sub-sections will be included in the new edition of ISO 9002.

4.2.1 General

The standard explicitly states that the documented quality system is made up of a quality manual and procedures. Additional wording states that the outline structure of the documentation covering the quality system requirements of this international standard shall be defined in a quality manual. The quality manual shall include or reference the documented procedures that form part of the quality system.

The new standard has made the duties of the management representative clearer, particularly the responsibilities of reporting to management on the performance of the quality system.

4.2.2 Quality System Procedures

A new paragraph after the present 4.2 (a) and (b) states that "the degree of documentation required for procedures that form part of the quality system shall depend upon the methods used, skills needed and training acquired by personnel involved in carrying out the activity".

This new section clarifies that it is not necessary to develop procedures for each and every process carried out by a company. Documented procedures need only exist where skills, training and methods have sufficient complexity or variation that risks are involved in not having adequate instructions to those performing the work. To some extent this is already addressed in process control where instructions are only required if their absence would adversely affect quality.

4.2.3 Quality Planning

More emphasis is placed on quality planning in the new standard as the supplier is now required to "define and document how the requirements for quality will be met. Quality planning shall be consistent with all other requirements of the supplier's quality system and shall be documented in a format to suit the supplier's method of operation."

The notes (a) to (g) of 4.2 have also been included as a requirement rather than a note and an additional sub-clause added for "the identification of suitable verification of appropriate stages in the product realisation".

The note was used in the 1987 edition to guide the supplier on what was necessary to plan for quality, the revised version specifies to the supplier what the minimum requirements are for quality planning.

4.3 Contract Review

The words "accepted tender" and "order (statement of requirement)" have been added to the term "contract" as an expansion or clarification of what must be reviewed. This clarification appears to be defining a contract as an accepted tender and/or order, all of which are to be considered as equal terms.

To cater for situations where a request for the supply of product is not in written form from the customer, an addition to 4.3.2 (a) states that "where no written statement of requirement is available for an order received by verbal means, the supplier shall ensure that the order requirements are agreed before their acceptance".

The standard clearly permits verbal orders which only need to be agreed (presumably verbally). Excluding across-the-counter sales, we believe an order should be documented by one of the parties to fulfil all the other requirements of the standard.

Amendments to contracts (contract variations) have been added to the standard. Amendments must be controlled so that information in the variation is passed onto the functions responsible for planning quality and performing the work. The wording states that "the supplier shall identify how amendments to a contract is made and currently transferred to functions concerned within the supplier's organisation".

A note in the standard defines a contract as "an agreement between supplier and customer transmitted by any means". This, therefore, allows orders to be verbal, written, hand delivered, posted, faxed or transmitted by any other electronic method.

4.4 Design Control

This element is included as a heading possibly to allow ISO 9001 and ISO 9002 to become one standard in the future. The new version states that "design control is outside the scope of this international standard".

4.5 Document Control

Four additions have been made to the existing text.

(i) It is made clear that this element of the system includes externally produced documents such as drawings and standards. The supplier must therefore review and approve documents supplied from the customer to meet specified requirements prior to them being issued.

(ii) A note has been added to the "general" clause that documents can be transmitted in any form to and from a supplier in hard copy, electronic or any other media.

(iii) The clause relating to the control of obsolete documents has included "invalid" documents which previously had to be removed and has the words "now may be otherwise assured against unintended use" added.

The current version requires obsolete documents to be removed and it is quite apparent that documents such as shop drawings may need to remain at a location until the end of a contract. The revision allows obsolete documents to be clearly marked (e.g. stamped superseded) and left at the location where they were being used.

(iv) An additional clause has been added that "obsolete documents retained for legal and/or knowledge preservation purposes should be suitably identified". Such documents which will not be used can be marked "for reference purposes only".

4.6 Purchasing

The two changes to the existing text relate to the assessment of subcontractors and supplier verification at the subcontractors' premises.

The last section of the existing 4.5.2 has been removed and the second paragraph has been extended to state that the control of subcontractors shall also be dependent upon "the impact of the subcontractor's product on the quality of the final product". This means that the controls placed on the suppliers of parts which have very little influence on the final product need not be as extensive as those suppliers of parts which have an important impact on the final work. The amount of control should be decided as part of the planning process when, for example, bills of material are being prepared and subcontractors selected. The amount of control will also be dependent upon the results of subcontractor assessment.

The second change is a new clause relating to the supplier's verification at the subcontractor's premises. It states that "where the supplier verifies purchased product at the subcontractor's premises, the supplier shall specify verification arrangements and the method of product release in the purchasing documents". This means that if the supplier wishes to inspect the subcontract work, then the method of product examination should be clearly described to the subcontractor.

4.7 Control of Customer-supplied Product

The term "purchaser" has been replaced by "customer".

4.8 Product Identification and Traceability

The main change to the standard is that "documented" procedures are now required for product identification and traceability whereas the previous version did not explicitly require procedures to be documented. It seems the new version has confirmed that procedures should be documented.

4.9 Process Control

Three changes to the existing text have been made and the element split into three separate paragraphs.

(i) The term work instruction has been replaced in section (a) by the term "work procedures" to eliminate the notion that there are numerous tiers of documents. The ruling is that there is no difference between a procedure and an instruction, both being defined as a step-by-step method of performing an activity.

(ii) The second clause combines (b), (c) and (d) to become (d), (e) and (f) respectively, and a new section (g) states "suitable maintenance of equipment to ensure continuing process capability".

There is currently no requirement in ISO 9002 for a company to keep its process equipment in good working condition. Preventive maintenance programmes should be part of a good quality management system to prevent the occurrence of nonconformance and the drift of product from established tolerances because of poorly maintained machinery.

(iii) The entire section on "special processes" has been removed, although the wording has been included as part of the section headed "process control". The main change to special processes is that "qualified operators" have been specified as the persons responsible for carrying out these special processes.

An additional requirement has been included which cross-references to the training element. This states that "the requirements for any qualification of process operations including associated equipment and personnel shall be specified". This clause means that during the planning phase of work, the supplier must pre-determine where it is necessary for personnel and equipment to be qualified. This will be a point where training requirements are identified and should be a consideration during Contract Review.

4.10 Inspection and Testing

(i) A new requirement which precedes the three inspection and test points has been added to the new version of the standard which states that "the supplier shall establish and maintain documented procedures for inspection and testing activities in order to verify that the specified requirements for a product are met. The required inspecting and testing and the records to be established, shall be documented in the quality plan or documented procedures."

This new requirement states that inspection and testing is to be controlled via documented procedures and specific points of inspection and the records to be maintained as specified in the contract must be detailed in documentation.

(ii) The note in the receiving inspection and testing clause has become an integral part of receiving inspection, thereby becoming a requirement rather than an informative note. Although the note has been included, there is no requirement to comply with it as it is more of a guidance or clarification paragraph.

(iii) The in-process inspection and testing section (b) of the current version has been deleted in its entirety as this requirement is already addressed in process control.

(iv) Finally, in the inspection and test records clause, there is a statement that "where the product fails to pass any inspection and/or test the procedures for control of nonconforming product shall apply" and "reworks shall identify the inspection authority responsible for the release of product".

The new version of the standard has now specified how to handle inspections and/or tests which have failed to meet specified requirements by using the nonconforming product system. Also, those authorised to release product need to be addressed in any inspection and test plan or within the various procedures used in this system element.

4.11 Inspection, Measuring and Test Equipment

Two minor additions to this system makes "software" an item to be included in measuring and test equipment and in the existing sub-clause (b) equipment can be calibrated and "adjusted" at prescribed intervals against certified equipment having a known relationship to national and/or "internationally" recognised standards.

These minor changes regarding software, equipment adjustment, and compliance with international standards are self-explanatory and in no way alter the original intent of the requirements.

4.12 Inspection and Test Status

The revised standard now requires that documented procedures and/or a quality plan must define the method of indicating the inspection status of a product which has passed or failed inspections. Previously there was no explicit requirements for procedures to exist.

4.13 Control of Nonconforming Product

The only change to this system is that repaired or reworked items can be reinspected against the "quality plan" in addition to or as well as documented procedures.

4.14 Corrective and Preventive Action

This element of the revised standard has been retitled to include "preventive action" in addition to corrective action.

Whilst preventive action was always included in the 1987 version of ISO 9002 the revised version has clearly separated the two activities and made a number of changes to enhance the specified requirements.

Corrective Action

Revised requirements include the "effective handling of customer complaints and reports of nonconformities" and the investigation of the cause of not only product but "process and quality system nonconformities". The "result of investigations have to be recorded" and the supplier must now "determine the corrective action needed to eliminate the cause of the nonconformity".

Preventive Action

This is a new section to the standard. Although preventive actions were previously specified, the following requirements must now be addressed.

"Procedures" need to exist for preventive action which must include "the use of appropriate sources of information", which in addition to the existing list must now include processes and work operations "which affect product quality" and "audit results".

The information or data which is collected has to be "analysed" so that potential causes of nonconformities can be eliminated. This proactive action to spot a problem before it exists can be facilitated by the use of control charts which can detect a trend towards product slipping out of conformance.

Major changes to this system include the "determination of the steps needed to deal with any problems requiring preventive action", "initiating preventive action and applying controls to ensure that it is effective" and for "ensuring that relevant information on actions taken including changes to procedures is submitted for management review".

4.15 Handling, Storage, Packaging, Preservation and Delivery

Sub-paragraph 4.15.4 has been made applicable to both "packing" and packaging, thereby clarifying the existing requirements.

4.16 Control of Quality Records

The title of this system has been changed to the "control of" quality records. The system requires procedures to be "documented" and must now include the "access" to quality records.

A note to the revised standard states that records can be in hard copy, electronic or other media.

4.17 Internal Quality Audit

There are three alterations to the revised standard. Firstly, it is a requirement for "audits to be carried out by personnel independent of those having direct responsibility for the activity being audited".

The second change is that corrective actions raised during the audit must be "followed up to confirm and record the implementation and effectiveness of the corrective action". The existing standard requires follow-up but does not explain what follow-up consists of.

Finally, internal quality audits shall be carried out by a supplier who has "established and maintained documented procedures for the planning and implementing of internal quality audits".

4.18 Training

The training system should follow "documented" procedures.

4.19 Servicing

A major change to the revised version of ISO 9002 is the inclusion of servicing control, which was an element previously included in ISO 9001. The standard has not changed in its revision from ISO 9001 and the requirement is that "where servicing is a specified requirement then procedures should be established and maintained. The procedures should include performing, reporting and verifying that services meet contract requirements."

4.20 Statistical Techniques

The supplier is now required to "identify the need" for statistical techniques and a sentence has been added to the requirements "where procedures to implement and control the application of statistical techniques are required".

The above changes are expected to appear in the 1994 issue of ISO 9002, although at the time of writing this section no guarantee is made that last minute changes to the standard will not occur.

INDEX

A

C

D

E

G

H

I

J

M